W9-ADC-320

THE SCULPTURE OF NEGRO AFRICA

The
SCULPTURE
of NEGRO
AFRICA

by PAUL S. WINGERT

COLUMBIA UNIVERSITY PRESS

MORNINGSIDE HEIGHTS · NEW YORK

THE PLATES INCLUDED IN THIS VOLUME

WERE FIRST PRINTED

IN THE CATALOGUE OF A LOAN EXHIBITION

OF AFRICAN NEGRO SCULPTURE

AT THE M. H. DE YOUNG MEMORIAL MUSEUM

GOLDEN GATE PARK, SAN FRANCISCO, CALIFORNIA

SEPTEMBER 24–NOVEMBER 19, 1948

First printing 1950
Second printing 1951

COPYRIGHT 1950, COLUMBIA UNIVERSITY PRESS, NEW YORK

PUBLISHED IN GREAT BRITAIN, CANADA, AND INDIA BY GEOFFREY CUMBERLEGE

OXFORD UNIVERSITY PRESS, LONDON, TORONTO, AND BOMBAY

MANUFACTURED IN THE UNITED STATES OF AMERICA

PREFACE

FORTY-ODD YEARS AGO a group of young artists "discovered" in a *bistro* in Paris a few pieces of African Negro sculpture. In their search for new forms, these artists, who were rebelling against traditional European art, were the first to recognize the aesthetic qualities in these primitive carvings. African Negro sculpture is now universally accepted as one of the world's great sculptures. This book is an introduction to that art—to its forms and their meaning and the purposes they were made to serve.

During the short time that this art has been known, many articles and books have been written on it and numerous collections have been assembled by museums and individuals in Europe and America. But the greater number of these objects had already been collected before the end of the past century, some of them as long ago as the latter part of the fifteenth century, by traders, explorers, and, more recently, by ethnologists. These carvings were looked upon, however, mainly as curios or as scientific specimens of primitive handicraft. The many examples in ethnological museums and family libraries or storerooms were considered crude fumblings by "savages" with no artistic merit. It was only after their aesthetic qualities had been discovered by the artists in Paris that these African objects were recognized as exemplifications of an important art.

The early writings and exhibitions dealing with this art stressed only its aesthetic features. No concern was given to the people who had created it or to the cultural environment that had nurtured it. But the appreciation of any art is greatly enhanced by an understanding of the meaning and uses of its forms and by some knowledge of the setting in which it flourished. This is particularly true of an art with a cultural background as different from our own as that of Negro Africa. In the present book, therefore, the art is examined, whenever possible, in its relationship to African institutions, beliefs, and ideas in order to add to the greater appreciation of its aesthetic qualities.

Negro sculpture is of special interest today because of the role it has played in the complex drama of modern art. It has served essentially to confirm the pioneering efforts of those artists who were seeking to revitalize art and to inspire them further towards the development of a nonrepresentational art. The value of this contribution, which is still continuing today, was considerable, and, although often overemphasized, should not be minimized.

The following text treats African art under the headings of the four art-producing geographical regions—West Africa, Cameroon, Central Africa, and East Africa. Within each of these regions the various major art areas are defined and important tribal styles are characterized. It is believed that the arrangement of the material in this way will help to make possible an understanding of specific styles and their relationships and that it will contribute to an appreciation of the richness and variety of forms in African art.

The vignettes in the text are intended to supplement the plates in order to make as clear as possible the essential characteristics of every style discussed. The examples illustrated by the plates are all in American collections and serve, in addition, to show the comprehensiveness and high aesthetic quality of African Negro art collections in this country. In every case credit for illustrations is due the museum or the person in whose collection the object belongs.

For advice and pertinent suggestions special thanks are due Dr. Marian W. Smith, of Columbia University, and Dr. Ralph Linton, of Yale University. The following institutions by generously placing their facilities at the author's disposal, have also contributed to the present work: the American Museum of Natural History, New York City; Brooklyn Museum; Buffalo Museum of Science; Chicago Natural History Museum; Museum of Modern Art, New York City; Newark Museum; New York Public Library, New York City, the Schomburg Collection; Peabody Museum, Harvard University; Peabody Museum of Salem, Mass.; Peabody Museum, Yale University; Royal Ontario Museum of Archaeology, Toronto; and the University Museum of the University of Pennsylvania, Philadelphia. Ac-

knowledgment is likewise made to the following persons:
Miss Geraldine Bruckner, of the University Museum, Phila-
delphia; Miss Bella Weitzner, of the American Museum of
Natural History, New York; Mr. Rene d'Harnoncourt, of
the Museum of Modern Art, New York; Mr. Chauncey J.
Hamlin, Dr. Carlos E. Cummings, and Miss Virginia
Cummings, of the Buffalo Museum of Science; Dr. Donald
Scott and Dr. J. O. Brew, of the Peabody Museum, Harvard
University; Professor T. W. McIlwraith, of the University
of Toronto and the Royal Ontario Museum of Archaeology,
Toronto; Mrs. Fred Zimmern, of the Brooklyn Museum;
Dr. Dorothy Williams, of the Schomburg Collection of the
New York Public Library; Professors Melville J. Herskovits
and William R. Bascom, of Northwestern University,
Evanston, Ill.; Mr. Ralph C. Altman and Mr. William
Moore, of Los Angeles; Mr. Vincent Price, of Beverly Hills
Calif.; and Mr. Julius Carlebach and Mr. Charles B. Spen-
cer, Jr., of New York. The vignettes in the text were made
by Miss Alexandra Rienzi and Mr. Robert M. Watts.

PAUL S. WINGERT

Columbia University, New York
May, 1950

CONTENTS

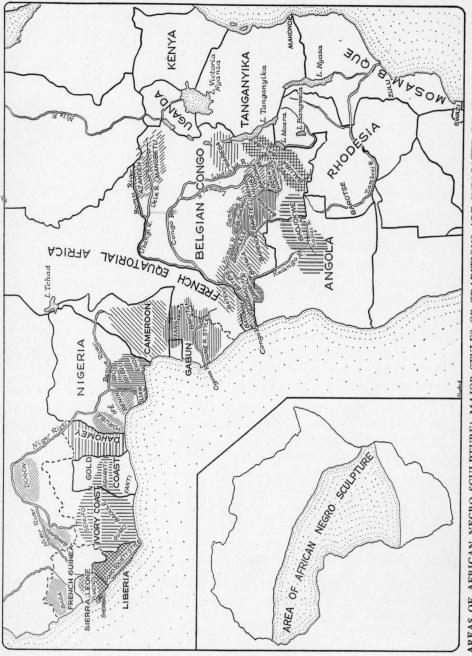

AREAS OF AFRICAN NEGRO SCULPTURE; MAJOR STYLES OR TRADITIONS ARE INDICATED BY SHADING

I THE SCULPTURE OF NEGRO AFRICA

For MANY CENTURIES before the Europeans began their conquest of the Continent, sculpture had occupied an important place in the life of the African Negro. A distinctive feature of their culture, in fact, was the use of sculpture in practically all ritual and ceremonies. Objects of everyday utility were also often enriched with carvings that were decorative and served no other purpose, while figures were sometimes carved solely for the aesthetic pleasure they gave. Sculpture varying in quantity and quality was produced by all the Negro peoples who had not been Mohammedized, for whom figure representation was forbidden. The art was therefore common over a vast area including the southern part of West Africa and continuing as a wide belt across Central Africa almost to the east coast.

Negro Africa has a dense population distributed among hundreds of tribes. Some of the larger tribes had a political organization so advanced that true kingdoms comparable to the early city states of Europe had been formed. Often the population is centered in large towns or even cities. Techniques were highly developed long before the coming of the Europeans to the Continent, and iron implements, in fact, were used both as weapons of war and as tools for the making of many objects, including sculpture. The great variety of cultures that were developed by the Negro emphasizes the extensive migrations and interminglings of peoples that had been going on for countless centuries. Yet a number of similar cultural elements are found throughout Negro Africa.

Among all peoples and in every era art is but one of the many facets of culture. In Africa these facets are often more closely interlocked than they are in our own civilization. Society, for example, has its basis in a stratified family that is composed of the husband at the head and his various wives, children, and retainers. But the family also constitutes a strong economic, political, and religious unit within itself. These comparatively small units are combined to form larger groups, the villages, which in turn are bound together into a still larger group, the tribe. The headman, or subchief, being leader of the village, and the paramount chief, or king, leader of the tribe, the organization of the larger units is similiar to that of the family. In some instances a number of tribes are banded together to form a nation under a king.

A man's rank and his position within the various units of his society are hereditary and are determined by the seniority of his birth. The chief, or king, is therefore the political, social, and often religious head of the tribe. An organized court life is centered around him. It includes the subchiefs, their retainers and those of the paramount chief, and the members of his advisory council. The tribe or nation controls a thorough system of taxation, supports a standing army, and maintains legal courts, which at times resort to trial by ordeal. It is also, due to the ceremonialism associated with court life, an important patron of the various arts and crafts.

Further patronage of artists and craftsmen accrues from ritual surrounding *ancestor worship,* the most widespread of African religious beliefs. The ancestors, through their environment in the spirit world, are the most important members of family, village, and tribe. They are cognizant of every act of their descendants and are at the same time in contact with the spirits of the more powerful ancient ancestors and with the gods. Hence they are in a position to aid or to bring misfortune on their descendants. Misfortune can be avoided by strict adherence to tradition and by rites conducted to honor or to petition the ancestors. Two classes of ancestors are worshiped—those of the tribe and those of the family. The tribal ancestors, who are the deceased kings, or chiefs, of the tribe, are the most powerful. With the living chief presiding, public rites are performed in

their honor for the welfare of the tribe as a whole. Family
ancestors are worshiped informally within the privacy of
their dwellings, where the family dead are petitioned on a
more individual basis. Works of sculpture are often
required for both public and private rites.

Other African religious concepts, centered in the worship of nature deities and belief in the efficacy of magic,
are responsible for the development of many local cults.
The *nature deities* are specialized gods who have control of
particular phenomena, such as birth, fertility of human
beings, crops, or animals, rain, lightning, and so forth.
Prayers and sacrifices, usually with a priest officiating, are
made to them. These deities are often represented by
carved figures. *Magic* is the belief that protection from
disease and other ills can be achieved through the use of
certain substances or objects in a particular way. The material agent through which magic is performed may be called
a *fetish*. The sculptor is frequently called upon to carve
a *fetish figure*, a carving to which magical materials are
added by a properly trained person, the "fetisher." It is
believed that the magical substances give the carving a soul
or a constantly present power and that this will act, when
properly petitioned, usually through the intervention of
the fetisher, as an intermediary to specific spirits in an effort
to attain the desired results.

Divination is a procedure developed in an effort to fore-
tell the future. The practice of it prevails throughout Africa
and has in some cases religious significance. In the hands of
a specialist, the diviner, it also requires the use of carved
objects.

The *secret society*, of great importance in many areas, is
another constant patron of the sculptor. It consists of an
organized group of men or women who perform, more or
less in secret, certain political, social, or religious acts. In
some tribes this institution is oppressive and greatly feared,
but in other tribes it functions for the public good. Frequently the most elaborate West African ceremonies are
performed by the secret societies. Some of them are designed
primarily to instruct the youth in the traditions of the tribe
and to instil in him, often forcibly, the proper conduct and

qualities that are expected of him as a member of adult society. Each secret society also has its own important ancestors and mythological or supernatural spirit helpers. With these, too, the youth is acquainted.

The African Negro depends largely upon agriculture for his subsistence. This is true for the forest-dwelling as well as for the open-grassland peoples. Trade, however, has always been an important feature of African culture. Large centers, often utilized by many tribes, are focal trading sites. It is documentary knowledge that trade included the basically decorative arts of the peoples using these centers, and since the decorative arts in almost all cases are similar to the more important major art forms, it is apparent that there was a good deal of intermingling of art styles. It is also evident that each tribe and often each village had its own particular style.

But certain common characteristics may be discerned in all African sculpture. With few exceptions the forms result from two almost equally important factors, namely, the sculptural tradition of the area, tribe, or village in which the artist lives and his powers of perception of the life about him. His forms in wood, metal, or ivory express that life with an amazing vigor. But the Negro sculptor does not copy nature. Instead, since he is concerned with sculptural expression, not representation, he simplifies or distorts those forms that he considers significant and generalizes or entirely suppresses the details unimportant to him. Although the types and basic designs of his forms are largely fixed by tradition, the sculptor with ability and sensitivity is able to give his work the full power of his artistic conception.

The human figure is universally used as subject matter. It is generally carved or modeled in the round and is small, few examples measuring more than two feet and many less than six inches high. Wood is the favorite material, and the carved figure is usually painted in black or red monochrome, notable exceptions being the polychromed figures and masks of the Yoruba and certain Congo tribes. The total effect of a carving sometimes depends on various other materials that are attached to it, such as shredded raffia,

clay, shells, beads, ivory, metal, feathers, or even pieces of
leather.

Male and female figures are often carved for use in ancestor rites. The *ancestor figure* may serve as an abode for
the spirit of the deceased, or it may be made in memory of
the dead. *Commemorative figures* in some areas seem to
have no religious significance. Elsewhere, offerings and petitions are made to both types of ancestor carving in the
belief that the spirit of the dead will come to the aid of the
living. The carved figure is not worshiped in either case,
but acts as an intermediary through which the spirit of the
ancestor is contacted.

Fetish figures are seldom carved with the same care as
are ancestor figures and are, with certain exceptions, smaller.
Some of them are set up in huts intended for that purpose
and are the property of the community, each with its own
fetisher who knows the prescribed method of activating the
power or spirit of the fetish. Others are the personal property of the fetisher or of individuals. In many regions, small
figures, when properly treated by a fetisher or by a sorcerer,
are carried, worn, or handled as charms to ward off evil
or to bring good fortune.

In some areas of West Africa the sculptured human form
represents or has become a traditional symbol of a god.
Formal petitions and sacrifices are addressed to the carving.
Among some tribes a similar type of figure is carved to
represent a god or to serve as a commemorative or ancestor
figure. It is often impossible to determine, in the absence of
specific information, to which category these figures belong.

In many parts of Africa utilitarian objects, such as house
posts, neck rests, stools, weaving pulleys, and various uten-
sils, are frequently decorated with human figures carved in
the round or in relief. Many ritual or ceremonial objects,
including divination vessels, drums, gongs or bells, bowls,
staffs, knives, and axes, are similarly decorated. Some of
these carvings also have a symbolic significance.

The mask is an art form used almost universally in Africa.
Although human features are the basic motivation for the
mask, many designs are based on animal heads, and some on
abstract forms. Used primarily in secret-society rites, the

mask may represent an ancestral or mythological spirit, and in a few areas it is set up and used in place of a fetish figure.

There are four principal types of masks: the face type, worn over the face; the helmet mask, fitting either partially or entirely over the head and resting on the shoulders of the wearer; the standard type, carved with a long or short handle, by which it is held before the face or above the head; and a headpiece type, worn on top of the head. Often costumes of raffia and other materials envelop the body of the wearer and hide his identity. In many instances the masked person is thought to be the incarnation of the spirit represented or symbolized by the mask. During the rites he may therefore speak with a disguised voice and generally conduct himself in a traditionally prescribed manner. Some masks may not be seen, under penalty of death, by anyone not a member of the secret society. Others are worn publicly when everyone participates in or witnesses the dances. But the meaning and use of many masks are not fully known to us, since the knowledge has never been divulged outside the society.

Although animal forms appear commonly in African art, they are much less extensively used than are human forms. They are often carved in the round as divination and fetish figures and as symbolic or decorative forms on ceremonial and utilitarian objects. The animal represented has for certain tribes and secret societies a religious or sociological significance. Animal forms are also frequently found in the rich vocabulary of surface decoration developed by some tribes. Carved in high or low relief, human as well as animal forms often combine in this decorative art with geometric designs that are derived from weaving patterns. These geometric motives are sometimes given names, and in some instances they have symbolic meaning. Much of the decorative art, however, is applied solely to enhance the beauty of an object and to make it worthy of being used by a person of high rank.

Man and the life about him provide, with few exceptions, the basic forms for African sculpture. But, because of the differences in culture, these forms vary considerably.

The area or tribe from which a work originates may therefore frequently be determined on the basis of the character
of its forms.

Style in a work of sculpture is the sum total of a number
of factors. These include the proportioning and shaping of
parts and the design or arrangement of them to express
certain relationships, the concept of form as volume or
mass, the treatment of surfaces, and the rendering of detail.
There are a great number of styles in African sculpture.
Each tribe and often each village, in fact, has its own style.
But, important similarities in the sculpture of neighboring
tribes may indicate that they share a single style tradition
within which their own tribal styles have developed. A
number of traditions, each represented by several tribal
interpretations, may be distinguished in the sculpture of
Negro Africa. The number of traditions and the variety
of styles that grew out of them indicate the vast scope of
African sculpture. Although relationships are apparent in
certain traditions, it is not possible to crystalize an African
style. But it is possible to discover a number of common qualities that contribute toward the aesthetic effects
achieved by this sculpture.

In most cases the African Negro artist is a professional
craftsman who has served an apprenticeship. Sometimes he
is also a fetisher, a sorcerer, or a priest. Sculpture is in some
tribes a hereditary vocation; in others, it is a matter of
talent and choice. In every area the artist works within
the tradition of his tribe. He is practically everywhere
esteemed socially, and in some tribes he has an important
political or religious status. The position of the artist in
his society and the demands placed upon his services reflect,
in general, the comparative economic security enjoyed in
many African tribes that allows the leisure necessary for the
creation and enjoyment of art.

Iron tools are used throughout Negro Africa. The basic
carving tool is the adze, although the knife, the scraper,
and the chisel are also used. During the apprenticeship of
the sculptor he learns not only how to use his tools but
also how to make them. Specialized carving tools have been
evolved in certain areas. A sculptor teaches his apprentice

all the improvements in the shaping of tools and the rendering of traditional designs that he has learned from experience.

The dating of African sculpture is, within limits, uncertain. For the majority of examples the only date that can be established is when the object was acquired, either in Africa or from a European or American dealer. In the latter case, the date means very little; but an African date has some significance. On the basis of the voracious habits of termites and the humid climatic conditions, it has been estimated that few wooden objects are more than fifty years old when they are purchased in Africa. Most African sculptures in our collections would therefore date between 1825 and 1890. Some examples, however, such as the Benin bronzes of West Africa and a few ivory carvings, can be dated as early as the fifteenth or sixteenth centuries.

From some regions of Africa the art of sculpture has disappeared. Disruption of the native culture, with the attendant destruction of those institutions that patronized the sculptor, has largely been responsible for this loss. But in many other areas, especially in Liberia, Yoruba, Dahomey, and Cameroon, the art continues with much of its former vigor.

The aesthetic qualities of African art are purely sculptural. Whether he was working in wood, or metal, the Negro artist gave his forms an existence in space so complete that as one moves around the often small objects, every changing silhouette adds to one's comprehension of the form. Only from all the silhouettes can the truly three dimensional conception of the artist be fully understood. His forms, although they are sculptural realizations or interpretations of nature, are not restricted by the limitations of realism. They are, instead, creative, and the functioning of each part is made clear by simplified, sometimes geometric shapes. Each work, consequently, has its complete existence as a sculptural form, not as a representation or simulation of nature. Each work also has a complete integrity of purpose—it was made with a specific meaning to serve a specific purpose that was seldom individual but was shared by all members of a group. The work, therefore, becomes expressive of the culture of the group as a whole, and is not merely the expression of an individual within the group.

Nevertheless, the individual ability and sensitivity of the sculptor is as important in African sculpture as it is in sculpture of all other countries and ages. This is evident in the recognition that some works are far superior in quality and expressiveness to others; they are masterpieces. The range of quality, however, is generally wide, wider, certainly, in some tribes than in others. A sureness pervades the work of the African Negro sculptor, with comparatively little evidence of virtuosity. Control and restraint mark the finest examples and give evidence of that sureness—nothing appears to be there that should not be, and nothing could be added. The work is complete in itself. It has its own existence in space, and its aesthetic qualities are purely sculptural.

II WEST AFRICA

AT ONE TIME sculpture flourished throughout Negro West Africa. The art is continued today in only a few regions. This change is to a large extent the result of prohibitions placed on many tribal customs subsequent to European domination in the second half of the nineteenth century. The introduction of cheap European trade goods also unfortunately led to the abandonment of certain native crafts. But there are many examples of the old art from this area in museums and private collections. Therefore, on the basis of these examples it is possible to recognize styles and designate art areas.

West Africa may be divided culturally and aesthetically into two parts: the Sudan to the north, a region of open grassland and rocky wastes, and the Guinea Coast to the south, a wide zone of light and heavy tropical forests. In both of these large areas the many linguistic and tribal groups have a number of basic cultural features in common, such as religious beliefs, secret societies, ceremonies, and types of wood sculpture. There is also a marked diversity of cultural elements that have resulted from many migrations and an intermingling of different peoples. During the past nine centuries a number of strongly organized states prospered and disappeared. Extensive areas and often diverse peoples were welded into empires, such as those of Ghana in the tenth century and Melle in the fourteenth century. Several West African kingdoms, notably Ashanti and Dahomey, existed as late as the nineteenth century.

Five major art areas can be distinguished in West Africa. These are the Sudan, the West, the Central, and the East Guinea Coast, and the Niger River Delta areas. Dahomey should be added to these as a separate art area, although it is somewhat transitional between those of the Central and those of the East Guinea Coast. In most cases the distinctive style elements of each area appear in the sculpture of several tribes. Important similarities are often apparent in the art of adjacent areas, and some tribal styles are composites of those found in several areas. The variety and distribution of art forms in West Africa are obviously the result of migrations and the diffusion of cultural elements; but the fact that many of these art styles show common basic principles indicates how comparatively few sculptural traditions were developed in this part of Africa.

THE SUDAN (A strongly defined art tradition is characteristic of the western portion of the vast region of the Sudan. The art area includes the territory within the great bend of the Niger River and along its upper reaches.) Five tribal styles best represent Sudanese sculpture: that of the Bambara, who live in the upper part of the Niger River system; that of the Mossi, east and southeast of the Bambara; that of the Dogon, who live south of the bend of the Niger; that of the Bobo, slightly southwest of the Dogon; and that of the Baga, a migratory people who now live on and near the coast of French Guinea. The tradition manifested in these five tribal styles consists of highly formalized human figures, and animal and human masks carved in wood, many of the forms and details having a geometric character. The sculptures are typified by an open design of slender, often elongated, forms that are posed with an almost rigid frontality and have strong interrelationships. Color is used sparingly and appears either decoratively or descriptively on only a few groups of masks.

The Bambara tribal style is one of the most spectacular and interesting aesthetically of the entire Sudan. This tribe, related linguistically to the Malinke and the Kassonke, developed a strong kingdom in the eighteenth and nineteenth centuries. Essentially agriculturists, they live in small villages, and have retained in a region subjected to strong Islamic influences the majority of their so-called paganistic beliefs.

Bambara religion is basically animistic. A great number of spirits, both good and bad, have their own particular character, their rituals, priests, and sacrifices. The good are emissaries of a supreme creator god and are petitioned to aid the supplicant, while the evil spirits, in conflict with the supreme being, are petitioned negatively, not to do harm. Ancestor worship is also an important Bambara religious belief.

A number of human figures, either male or female, are carved in wood for use in ancestral and animistic rites. They range in size from two to thirty inches high. Wooden masks of various designs are used more commonly, however, in religious ceremonies. Masks are used mostly by secret societies that are essentially confraternities or groups of men bound together under the aegis of a particular spirit or spirits. Strict rules determine the conduct of these societies, and the nature of the rites they perform, some of which are carried out secretly and some publicly. Not all of these rites are religiously motivated, but some are of judiciary or social significance. The importance of these secret societies is therefore very great and far reaching. Comparatively few other ritual objects are carved, and very little purely decorative sculpture is produced.

A distinctive type of figure carving is characteristic of the Bambara style (Pls. 1–3). Simplified structural parts are marked off with precise clarity and are distorted so that the proportions, through the slender tapering torso and its continuation in the long thin neck, dramatize a verticality and lead the eye to the protruding volumes of the breasts and finally to the large projecting head. The outline is clear and emphatic from whatever angle the figure is viewed. Sharp angles, sudden changes in direction, and a few curves allow it to create a moving line pattern in space. The heavy forms of the head, breasts, and animal-like hands are attached with careful equilibrium to the slimmer supporting columnar torso and neck. These in turn carry the weight down to the legs and feet. The effect is one of stolidity, yet lightness. Surfaces are smoothly carved, and geometric descriptive details, cut deeply into the surface, are confined to a few areas. The head is typical of Bambara style. Large features are distributed over the entire area of the narrow flat facial planes and are dominated by the huge

nose that projects with a high straight bridge from a narrow receding forehead. The chin is also abruptly receding.
The sides and top of the head are decorated with deeply
cut high-relief designs and an elaborate coiffure with delicate low-relief carving.

Three types of Bambara masks are used extensively. Simplified animal heads, many of them representing the hyena,
are worn in the public and secret rites of the Kore society
(Pl. 6). Smooth and undecorated surfaces define boldly
contrasting rounded and flattened forms that are contained
within a continuous outline. These masks represent benevolent spirits that are controlled by this society. A more
complicated type of face mask is used in the rites of a
confraternity of seven- to eight-year-old boys who are
banded together under a group of protective spirits (Pl. 5).
The mask represents the N'tomo spirit that protects the
boys against evil and insures them of strength and health.
The design consists of a narrow, typically stylized Bambara
face, topped by two, four, or more straight horns, often
with a small figure standing between them. The effect is
that of an elaborate open-work top above the solid forms
of the face below. Surfaces are usually smoothly carved,
with a few lightly incised linear details.

The most spectacular Bambara mask is the Tji'Wara
(Pl. 4). This is a highly stylized antelope or antelope head,
often more than two feet high, that is always carved in an
open-work or pierced design. It is mounted on a woven
wicker cap and is worn on top of the head by a dancer
who imitates the leaping of an antelope. The Tji'Wara
mask represents both male and female evil spirits that the
wearer seeks to propitiate at sowing and harvest seasons so
that harm will not befall the crops. No two of these masks
have the same design, but they all have similar style elements, such as rhythmic and often balanced patterns of
elegant curvilinear forms that are frequently decorated
with incised geometric surface designs. These masks are
given a great richness of design by the movement and
countermovement of graceful curving lines interspersed oc-
casionally with sharp angular forms.

The Dogon tribal style is equally characteristic of Sudan

art. These people live in a rocky forbidding region near the bend of the Niger River. They are farmers and hunters who migrated probably a long time ago from the south. The Dogon carve figures and many masks to use in the complex religious rites of their various ancestor and totemic cults. Some of their sculpture, as is that of the Bambara, is made by the blacksmith caste, which is a powerful, specially privileged group. The Dogon also carve decoratively certain ritual and utilitarian objects, such as large wooden urns and doors. Their style lacks the elegance of line and the refinement of surface detail that the Bambara has and depends more upon the bold contrast and balancing of carved shapes. Masks are frequently painted red, black, white, or yellow, and at times small schematic representations of the masks are painted on the stone walls of certain caves.

The Dogon carve various types of figures, male, female or hermaphroditic, some seated, others standing (Pls. 7–8). A striking feature of this style is the complete balancing of three dimensional forms, not only those of one side with the other, but also the forms of the back with those of the front. The projection of the beard, for example, is balanced by that of the hair at the back of the head, the breasts by the shoulders, and the thighs by the buttocks. In the older examples (Pl. 7), the body forms are often thin and elongated, the square-jawed head tapers to a sharp, narrow cranium, and the eyes and mouth are horizontal diamonds carved in high relief. The design discloses a closed and often static form, although it is sometimes compact, sometimes pierced. Dogon figures are used in fertility and ancestor funerary rites. In both cases they are made as recipients of the vital force, energy, or power of mythological, historic, or recent ancestors, so that this force may be acquired by or utilized for the benefit of the living. Fertility figures are frequently set up in the fields or in caves, and funerary figures are placed in sanctuaries, where sacrifices are periodically made to them.

A profusion of masks is characteristic of the art of this tribe. They represent in naturalistic or geometric shapes animals, birds, snakes, crocodiles, and human beings. They are used entirely by the men's religious confraternities. The greater number of their rites in which masks are worn are performed publicly for the common good, and they are not therefore actually secret societies. Many of these ceremonies are funerary, at the death of a member; others are in memory of important ancestors. Masks are, as are the figures, containers of the vital force or energy of the animal or person represented.

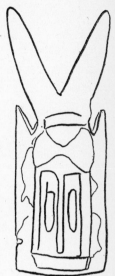

A wide variety of designs appear in Dogon masks, but many of them are variants of one basic design. The common shape is a vertical rectangle. The flat surface is divided vertically into five long, narrow rectangles, of which the second and the fourth are often deeply depressed. Very large triangular or rectangular eye openings are cut in these sunken areas. Many of the masks are roughly carved, and frequently their surfaces are painted with red triangles, red dots, or with flat areas of red, black, or white. A wide fiber ruff or fringe, often red, is worn with these masks. The surface painting and the ruff are representational or symbolic. Some of the masks are surmounted by carved human or animal figures, and others by geometric forms, often four or more feet high.

Frequently Dogon masks have an intensity of dramatic feeling in their carved shapes that is more expressive of life forms than the static, severe poses of their schematically designed figures.

The Mossi tribal style has numerous analogies with the sculpture of the Bambara and the Dogon. They carved comparatively few figures, but their masks are distinctive in design and have a fine aesthetic quality. Mossi masks consist of a stylized horned animal head, surmounted by a very tall, narrow palette. The upper part of the female masks is carved with a dramatically posed female figure that is sculptured almost entirely in the round and is adossed to a flat background of geometric shape. These figures have the typical attenuated forms and stylized shapes of Sudan art. The male masks are surmounted by much taller carvings that contain flat, often pierced, geometric designs which symbolize in a highly abstract way male figures. There is no suggestion in these male masks of naturalistic

form. Both kinds of mask represent particular types of
spirits controlled by various secret societies.

A fourth characteristic Sudan style was developed by the
Baga tribe. Little is known of the customs and beliefs of
these people who have now come under strong Moslem influence. Their art comprises standing male and female
figures carved in wood, drums supported by small free-
standing figures, and some of the most spectacular of all
West African masks. It is likely that Baga sculpture was
made for use by the Simo Society, a grade-society about
which little is known. The style combines a few simplified
naturalistic forms with a number of highly stylized, almost
abstract shapes.

Two types of figure were carved by this tribe. One is
statically posed, with the hands clasped under the chin
(Pl. 9), and the other is dynamically posed, the knees flexed
and the arms cut free from the body. Both types represent
the human figure in simplified, almost geometric forms that
are defined by smooth undecorated surfaces. In profile these
surfaces produce firm outlines. While Baga figures vary in
proportions, some short, others elongated, the torso is
always a full-volumed protruding form, often carved with
a projecting navel. The arms are sometimes integrated
with the shoulders, and in other examples they are carved
in high relief on the surface of the torso, with only the
forearms carved in the round.

The huge, highly stylized head is one of the most distinguishing features of this style. It surmounts a long,
columnar neck, from which, as in Bambara figures, the
entire head projects toward the front. The head is short,
narrow, and very deep. A low crest extends from the neck
to the forehead. This is continued as a vertical ridge across
the forehead and culminates in a huge hooked nose. The
face terminates in a sharp-pointed chin and is outlined
by a band of incised carving. Very large, partly closed,
heavily lidded eyes are set close to the nose; while the
planes of the face are meager flat surfaces. The sides of the
head are decorated with an elaborate incised pattern composed of chevrons and cross-hatched lines. Large animal-like
ears are placed near the back of the head. The expression

is calm, haughty, and aloof; and the design suggests bird,
animal, and human forms.

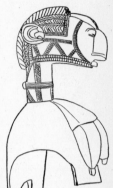

The Baga used a unique type of African mask. It consisted of a very large carved bust, the upper part of the
torso hollowed out so that it could be supported on the
shoulders of the wearer. The head and neck of these large
masks, some measuring more than three feet in height, are
identical in style to those of the figures, although the surface decoration is often more elaborate. These masks are
either male or female. The female ones are called "nimba"
and are said to be containers for maternity and fertility
spirits or powers. Another important type of Baga mask
is known as "banda." It, too, is a large mask and was worn
on top of the head of the wearer at a forty-five degree angle
toward the front. Its complex geometric design combines
crocodile, human, and antelope features. The human forms
consist of a small rounded forehead, from which a high
short nose develops, and an elaborate headdress, while the
crocodile resemblance is suggested by the very long sharp
jaws that project below the human features. Antelope horns
and ears complete the synthesis. In some examples the headdress and the sides of the face are decorated with incised
designs of chevrons and cross-hatchings; in others, triangular and chevron designs are carved in low relief and picked
out in red and white against a black background. The
"banda" masks were used in Simo Society rites and at death
ceremonies for members of the society. Nothing else is
known of the elements so richly stylized in their designs.

A fifth Sudan tribal style is represented by the various
masks used by the Bobo tribes. One type resembles in its
proportions and forms the "banda" masks of the Baga.
Other types have a tall superposed decorative carving similar to, but smaller than, those of Mossi masks. Some Bobo
masks are covered with painted triangular designs reminis-
cent of those appearing on certain Dogon masks. An animal-
head mask was also carved by these people, either with a
simplified naturalism or a dramatic stylization. Bobo masks
were used much as were those of the Mossi, although some
of them seem to have represented ancestral spirits and
others animal power.

The five major styles of the Sudan clearly manifest one basic tradition. The art is characterized by elaborate, highly stylized, almost abstract designs that are sometimes refined to the point of sophisticated elegance. Forms and designs are on an unusually large and impressive scale, while sharp contrasts in surface, shapes, and line often produce spectacular effects.

WEST GUINEA COAST   The West Guinea Coast art area embraces portions of the political divisions of Sierra Leone, Liberia, and the Ivory Coast. Two related styles are representative of the sculpture of this area, that of the Mendi tribe and that of the Poro Society. The latter includes the art of the various tribes among whom the Poro Society is paramount, and although there are many variations in the style of the masks used by this society, yet the existence of common design types makes it possible to recognize in this sculpture a basic style. There are certain similarities in the art of the West Guinea Coast area with that of the Sudan area, but these are combined with other elements that give to this sculpture its distinctive character.

The Mendi tribe, a numerous people of farmers and fishermen, live within the political limits of Sierra Leone. Their art is similar to that of neighboring tribes, who appear to have been strongly influenced by them. It consists of a few types of figures and masks and some decorated ritual objects. These sculptures are made for use by the strong secret societies that dominate the religious, social, and political life of the Mendi. The Bundu is one of the most important of these societies. Strictly a female secret society, it is devoted largely to the training of young girls so that they can assume adult responsibilities in tribal, particularly in the marital life.[1] The Yassi, also essentially a female society, functions primarily in the divination of the curability of the sick. All Mendi sculptures are painted a dull black and are carved in a style that shows little variation.

The large masks worn by the leaders of the Bundu Society

[1] The Poro, a powerful male secret society, also has wide distribution among the Mendi, from whom, in fact, it derives its name. For a discussion of the Poro Society see p. 20.

are the best-known sculptures of this tribe (Pl. 10). They
are shaped like a helmet and fit so as to cover the head of
the wearer entirely. There are many local village variations
within the style of Bundu masks, but they are all characterized by a number of distinctive features. The mask is dominated by an enormous, elaborately decorated headdress
and a huge bulbous forehead. The features of the face, often
diamond shape, are small in proportion and are placed very
low in the facial area. A sharply depressed line, formed by
the conjunction of the forehead and facial planes, frequently extends horizontally across the face through the eye
area and across the bridge of the nose. The whole design is
characterized by amplitude and defined by large smooth
rounded surfaces clearly separated by deeply indented lines.
These surfaces give the impression of active expansion,
and together with the over-all size of the headdress, they
produce an effect of heaviness.

Bundu masks represent the protective spirit of the society. They are worn with an enveloping costume of black
palm fiber, and the priestess wearing the mask carries a
short staff, frequently decorated with spiraling geometric
designs and carved heads (Pl. 11), that are simplifications of
those represented by the mask.

Mendi figures show two variants: one naturalistic; one
more geometric. Of these, the naturalistic type is the most
important aesthetically. Female figures are almost exclusively represented, often without a base and with slender
proportions that consist of strong naturalistic legs, elongated torso, and a very long neck. The forms are compact,
the arms often not cut free from the body, and anatomical
details, such as joints, rendered more structurally than they
are in Sudan figures. The neck and head are interesting
modifications of the stylized forms of the Bundu masks in
the direction of greater naturalism. A slight degree of life-
likeness, for example, appears in the carving of the cheek
bones and chins of the figures. Elaborately carved surface
designs are confined, as in the masks, to the headdress.

The majority of Mendi figures are used by the priestesses
of the Yassi Society as a medium through which the spirits
convey their decisions in response to divination rites. Half-

figures of like style were carved within a hollow bowl and
used by the Yassi Society among the Shebro Island [2] neighbors of the Mendi (Pl. 12).

A second style of the West Guinea Coast area appears in
the many masks of various types used by the Poro Secret
Society. This is a very distinctive and important West
African style that exerted considerable influence beyond
the limits of the area of which it is characteristic. Practically
all the tribes in this part of West Africa had the Poro Society
in one form or another. These include Mendi, Shebro,
Buzi, Mano, Da, Geh, Bassa, and many other tribes. Although the masks show many tribal and regional variations,
they are all variants of a number of basic types.

The Poro Society is, in its most developed form, a true
secret society. All male members of a tribe, before being
admitted to full tribal standing, have to belong to the
Poro. Membership is determined by rigorous initiation
rites that involve ordeals, instruction in tribal customs, the
cutting of tribal scarification marks on the body, and the
introduction to ancestral and supernatural spirits and gods
represented by masked figures. There are within the society
a number of grades or degrees. Throughout their lives men
strive constantly to elevate their standing in the society,
since the Poro controls, often oppressively, the social, political, and economic life of the people. The society is, moreover, intertribal, so that a man can participate at the proper
level in the rites of neighboring tribal groups.

Two types of masks are used by the Poro Society: one
is worn only within the precincts of the Poro house, and
the other in the public activities of the society. Both kinds
represent and contain the spirit of a god or of an ancestral
or supernatural being important to the society.

Three significant styles can be recognized among the
great variety of Poro masks. One is based on simplified
human features (Pl. 16), another is composed of heavy
geometric semi-human forms (Pl. 14), and a third represents
a greatly stylized, often geometric animal or human head
(Pls. 13, 15). Each type shows the development of one or

[2] The Shebro Islands lie near the coast of Sierra Leone, and their culture
is basically similar to that of the Mendi.

more elements that are characteristic of the Poro style.
These elements comprise a clear definition and separation
of component parts of the design, breadth of surface planes,
emphasis on carved shapes, volumes and forms, and an expression of space through the depth of form. All the designs
are completely bisymmetrical, and in many examples this
is greatly exaggerated.

Masks with simplified human features (Pl. 16) often have
a bisecting vertical ridge from the top of the forehead to
the bridge of the nose. This emphasizes the bisymmetry of
the design, but it also brings all parts of the design into a
close unity. The rounded, sometimes bulbous forehead
and the flattened area of the face are carved as a continuous
sensitive surface plane broken only by facial features.
There is expressed in this type of mask a marked feeling
for natural forms and shapes that in some instances ap-
proaches individual characterization.

The geometric semi-human Poro masks (Pl. 14) are
dramatic in appearance, often with an articulated, or
hinged, lower jaw that can be moved by the wearer. Human
features are interpreted by large-scale schematic forms,
such as projecting tubular eyes and cubistically carved
cheeks, having line demarcations and variations in depth.
The mouth is often a huge animalistic form; both jaws are
sometimes wrapped with fiber, and shells and seeds are frequently suspended from the underside of the movable lower
jaw. No surface decoration appears on these masks. They
are spectacularly sculptural because of the separation and
depth of their forms and the strong delineation of their
shapes.

The third type of Poro mask is in some respects a combination of the above two. In such examples as the sheep
(Pl. 15) and bird (Pl. 13) masks, stylizations of natural
forms often appear with marked geometric or cubistic
definition. But other masks of this group have little relationship with natural shapes. In common with the above
two types, this type is characterized by large-scale, clearly
defined forms, and by strongly carved surface planes.

The Poro style agrees with the Mendi in that its emphasis is on form and volume. Both styles are analogous to

that of the Sudan in their use of geometric forms and elaborate surface decoration. But the greater naturalism of the
West Guinea Coast art suggests an element foreign to that
of the Sudan, an element that becomes increasingly important in the art east of this area.[3]

CENTRAL GUINEA COAST   A distinguished art tradition developed in the Central Guinea Coast area, which embraces
substantially the political limits of the Ivory Coast and the
Gold Coast. Two closely related styles are evident in the
sculpture from this region. One appears in the carvings of
the Baoulé, Guro, and Senufo tribes, who live in the central, western, and northern portions of this area. The second style is expressed by the art of the Ashanti peoples of
the Gold Coast to the east. A striking similarity exists in the
forms and designs of the sculpture by the Baoulé, the Guro,
and the Senufo. Their art consists of figures, masks, and a
considerable amount of purely decorative carving. Wood
was the preferred material, although the Baoulé did cast a
number of small figures and masks in bronze, a medium
extensively used by the Ashanti, who did comparatively
little wood carving. From west to east the style of the Central Guinea Coast area is increasingly naturalistic.

The Baoulé are descendants of the Ashanti. They migrated into the region where they now live in the eighteenth
century, bringing with them a culture superior to that of
the indigenous peoples of this area, the Guro and the
Senufo. It appears, however, that the unique and homogeneous art developed by these three tribes was the result
of cultural interrelationships, not the contribution of the
Baoulé alone, since the art differs considerably from that
of the Ashanti. The most important style elements distinctive of this sculpture are refinement of form, surface, and
detail and an accomplished technical facility.

Numerous figures are carved by the Baoulé (Pls. 18–21).

[3] A number of steatite figures have been unearthed in the West Guinea
Coast area. These lie stylistically midway between the Mendi and Poro
sculptures, many of them near the strong naturalism of the Poro masks. It
seems unlikely, in spite of local traditions, that these stone carvings are
"ancient." They represent, in fact, another manifestation of the homogeneous elements in the art style of this area.

These measure from eighteen to twenty-four inches high, represent seated or standing male or female figures, and are carved in a hard, close-grained wood that is given a high polish and stained a monochrome red, gray, or black. Each figure varies in proportions and details, yet each carving reveals the elements of a common tradition. The most noteworthy characteristics of Baoulé figure style are the complete unity of the component elements of form, the importance of surface planes, and the preciseness of the high-relief rendering of details. Whether seated or standing, these sculptures are usually carved on a low circular base.

In these figures, slender, sometimes elongated proportions build up from short heavy legs that are carved in the round, often with an exaggerated curvature of the calves and buttocks (Pls. 18–21). The arms are held closely to the sides of the body and are seldom cut free; the hands are placed in front of or at the sides of the lower torso. A long heavy neck elevates and sets apart the large head. All the structural parts of the body, clearly and separately defined, are rendered as three-dimensional, often cylindrical forms. These are carved with smooth surface planes, which, although sometimes interrupted by the exaggerated demarcation of joints, flow from form to form and give to the entire figure a unity through the continuous surface treatment. The forms are rendered in the idiom peculiar to the village or region whence they are derived. Baoulé figures are sculptural transcriptions of life. This is clearly evident in the pose and in the formation of and the organic relationships between the various parts. But nature is not copied scientifically or visually. The structurally important forms and volumes are amplified or reduced to serve as sculptural rhythmic counterparts of and supports for the climatic and elaborately carved head. Few realistic details are carved on the body.

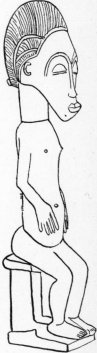

The head, as the focal part of the design of Baoulé figures, is carved with a profusion of descriptive detail. Various head shapes, coiffures, and scarification designs occur, but within these variations consistent style elements are readily apparent. The face is an elegant oval, wide, almost semicircular, above the forehead and narrow at the chin. A prognathism is often suggested by the projection of the face, and in male figures this is further emphasized by an elaborate, frequently long beard. Facial features and scarification designs are always carved in high relief. A heart-shape design is often contained within the oval of the face by joining the arched eyebrows with the bridge of the nose and fusing the outer curve of the eyebrows with that of the sides of the face. This effect is made clear by the long flat nose and the small mouth surmounting the small tapering chin. Smoothly finished surfaces flow easily into one another and subtly suggest volume rather than a bony structure. An elaborate linear pattern is given to the surface by the facial features and scarification marks. This reaches a climax in the carved designs that define the various forms of hairdress.

Baoulé figures are made to contain the spirits of the dead, as representations of gods, and as art objects esteemed for their aesthetic quality alone. Portraiture is spoken of in connection with some of these sculptures, but it is evident that this consists of slight variations within the traditional design and does not lead to an individual characterization.

The numerous masks carved by this tribe are based on human or animal features (Pl. 22). Refinement of form and technique distinguishes them from all other African masks. Some of those having human features resemble the facial forms of the Baoulé figures; in others the design is more stylized and is carved with even greater care than that of the figures. The male masks, for example (Pl. 22), frequently have a full beard stylized as a scalloped design that flanks the face and terminates in a short cylindrical pendant. Facial features are sometimes schematically rendered to produce a decorative pattern. Masks with human features are often surmounted by horns, birds, or human or animal heads that combine rhythmically with the designs below.

The animal masks usually represent short-horned ox heads. They too vary in design from the comparatively naturalistic to the more stylized. But the stylizations are unlike those of the animal masks of the Sudan and frequently result from a formalized treatment of human features adapted to the animal head.

The precise meaning and uses of many Baoulé and other Central Guinea Coast masks are unknown. Apparently some were worn in secret and public rites of religious societies; others seem to represent deities.

Guro and Baoulé masks and figures are frequently so similar that differentiation is difficult (Pls. 24–25). The majority of Guro sculptures, however, are characterized by more slender proportions and less decoratively carved facial features than are the Baoulé. Distinguishing features often found in their art are long, narrow obliquely slanting eyes, sometimes referred to as "oriental," and the elegantly carved zigzag design just above the high forehead.

Senufo art reflects the northerly location of these tribes. It is to some extent transitional between the Sudan styles and those of the Baoulé and the Guro. The sculpture of the more northern Senufo tribes is substantially Sudanese in style, while that of the southern groups is a simplified, often geometric rendering of basic Baoulé elements. Senufo figures (Pl. 26) are of short, often squat proportions. They are composed of geometric, compactly integrated shapes that have little surface or descriptive detail and thrust forward in a rhythmically balanced manner comparable to that of Sudan figures. Their masks represent human features, but lack the refinement of form and design of those of the Baoulé and the Guro (Pl. 27). Rectangular and half-oval projections appear at each side of the face, short stylized legs jut down from the chin, and human, bird, or geometric designs are carved on the head. Surface designs, such as eyebrows and scarification marks, usually consist of deeply cut parallel lines. Senufo masks give the impression of shallowness and thinness.

Decorative sculpture, both in the round and in relief, is highly developed by the Baoulé; less well by the Guro and the Senufo. The weaving pulley is the most commonly decorated object. Many of them are carved with human or animal heads or figures in the round and constitute characteristic examples of the Baoulé and the Guro style. Ritualistic and other ultilitarian objects, such as divination bowls, drums, gong mallets (Pl. 23) spoons, and combs, are also decoratively carved by these two tribes.

Artists are highly esteemed among the Baoulé and the Guro, and their reputation frequently spreads beyond the limits of their small villages. Their services are sought after, and men of rank sometimes secure examples of their work for no other reason than aesthetic pleasure. The appreciation of art for its own sake has thus produced a connoisseurship. Sometimes, in fact, a man may "exhibit his collection" in front of his house so that others may also enjoy it. Senufo sculptors are, like those of the Sudan, members of a craft caste and have religious and social position.

Small bronze-gold weights, cast by the cire-perdue process, are the most representative examples of Ashanti art. Surface gold was at one time fairly plentiful in the Ashanti area and was used in the form of gold dust as currency prior to and even after their contact with Europeans. These peoples developed in the eighteenth and early nineteenth centuries a strong kingdom that was not finally brought under British control as a protectorate until 1895. As the currency of the state, gold dust was a royal monopoly. A system of weights was devised that was based on a unit of value known as the "ackie," about one-sixteenth of an ounce. Thirty-five ackies formed an average series of weights. The majority of the weights were cast in bronze, a few of them in brass or copper. Weights of a particular size and value, however, were restricted to royalty or nobility. The weights were first modeled in beeswax before they were cast; the technique and the right to make them were inherited privileges of a few families. Each weight is unique, since no duplicates or casts are possible by the cire-perdue method.

Ashanti gold weights are of two kinds—animate forms and inanimate objects. In the first group, human figures, animals, birds, fishes, and insects are represented; in the second, plants, seeds, fruits, weapons, articles of daily use, and purely geometric designs (Pl. 29). Human figures often depict scenes of daily life, several of them frequently arranged in a group, for example, two gossiping women. Proverbs and religious subjects are also portrayed by human figures. In every case, the human form is drastically simplified and is executed with an active, almost impressionistic naturalism not found in other African Negro styles. These small figures, many less than two inches high, lack the refinement of form and detail of Baoulé sculptures. They are, in fact, roughly modeled. The subject matter became traditional and was consequently repeated again and again, but always as a new interpretation by the sculptor. The spontaneity of expression and the vitality of these small figures are unparalleled in African art. They live and move and have a vigor of reality that associates them closely with the life of the people.

Ashanti metal art, however, reaches its highest level in the small bronze urns or vessels (*kuduo*) that were made for ceremonial use (Pl. 30). They consist of a deep body and a hinged top, on which two fighting animals are usually represented in the round. The body of the vessel and often the animal forms are richly decorated with magnificently chased surface designs. Such urns were buried with the head of the family. Many of the *kuduo* in museums and private collections have been recovered from excavated graves.

Comparatively few wood carvings of the human figure were made by the Ashanti. They are best represented by the "Akua'Ba," small fertility figurines (Pl. 28). Half- or full-length male or female forms are represented by naturalistic or schematic shapes. The neck and the head, however, are always stylized, the neck as a long, slender form frequently ringed in a manner comparable to the Mendi figures, and the head flat and roughly circular. Front and back surfaces of the head are slightly convex, and a stylized pattern of continuous lines representing eyebrows, and nose is carved in high relief on the front. In other examples the facial features and the hair are indicated on the surface by incised lines. The high degree of stylization of the heads of Akua'Ba figures suggests comparison with Sudanese art, while the facial design is analogous to certain Baoulé masks.

Decorative sculpture is highly developed among the Ashanti. Various objects, such as spoons, combs, wooden plates, and calabashes, are carved with geometric surface designs. But the most important decorative carving appears on their wooden stools, which are carved from a single block of tough-fibered, heavy, light-colored wood. The general design is uniform, the details varying greatly, and con-

sists of a heavy rectangular base connected by vertical supporting members of different shapes and a long, deeply concave top. The central supporting stem, often cylindrical,
is entirely hollowed out from below, and is frequently
flanked by four slender supports, carved as geometric designs in the round.

The Ashanti stool has religious and social, as well as
purely utilitarian, significance. It is believed that the soul of
a man is closely connected with his stool. While the design
denotes the social and political position of its owner during
his lifetime, at death the stool becomes a shrine into which
the spirit of the deceased can be induced to enter during
certain ceremonies. Petitions and sacrifices are at that time
offered to the stool in honor and supplication of the ancestor. The Ashanti stool, therefore, serves in place of the
carved figures used in ancestral rites in other parts of West
Africa. Stools of important chiefs are greatly revered, but
the most sacred of all is the Golden Stool into which it is
believed the soul of the Ashanti nation has entered. This
stool was acquired miraculously from the sky in the early
eighteenth century and marked the beginning of this belief.

The roots of the art of the Central Guinea Coast area are
deeply embedded in a perceptive understanding of nature.
In the western part of the area it is marked by a controlled
naturalism that pervades the sculptured forms and in the
east by a less restrained expression of reality, with much of
the subject matter taken from daily life.

DAHOMEY   To the east, the art style of Dahomey is transitional. The art of this kingdom is centered in the royal city
of Abomey, but the state embraced a good portion of the
central area of the present political province of Dahomey
and the western and southwestern parts of Nigeria. It was
one of the outstanding royal arts of Africa. In the old days
brass casting, clay modeling, cloth appliquéing, and the
carving of calabashes were controlled by royalty or nobility.
Wood carving was the only democratic art that could be
patronized and acquired by everyone.

Originally Dahomean metal work was the product of a
restricted family guild whose members worked as retainers

of royalty or nobility. Human figures and animals were cast in brass. They are larger in size than the gold weights of Ashanti, but like them they were cast by the cire-perdue process. They represent scenes from daily life and the fauna of the country (Pl. 31a). Figures are frequently arranged in groups, such as the representation of a chief and his retinue traveling. Animals are either naturalistic (Pl. 31a) or fantastic. Both human and animal forms are slender, often elongated, and the surfaces are frequently carefully chased with designs indicating the pelt of an animal or the details of a costume. Movement, usually suggested by an arrested pose, is an important element in the style of these small brass figures. They serve no other purpose than to give aesthetic pleasure to those who can afford to own them. They have, however, a sociological significance, since the possession of them indicates a certain affluence and social position.

Clay relief modeling was also in the past a restricted art. It was used only to decorate the walls of royal palaces and the compounds of nobility. These decorations consist of small square panels within which important historical events are represented by high-relief modeling. The composition usually contains two figures of short, heavy proportions, with large round heads that are painted red, white, and black. These figures are rendered by a simplified naturalism showing only a few descriptive details. Movement is also indicated, as in the brass castings, by momentary poses.

The more democratic art of wood carving consists of figures and ceremonial objects, although scepters were carved for kings and chiefs (Pl. 31b). With the exception of the scepters, the greater portion of wood sculpture was made for religious uses. Figures with human form are made as a means of contacting certain gods. They are set up in a shrine, and petitions and offerings are directed to the god through the medium of the figure. Many wooden figures are also carved as containers of specific supernatural powers through which the gods cure or protect mankind. These figures are sometimes carved by professional sculptors, but they are often made by the person who needs them, whether he is a skilled wood carver or not, since this avoids the risk of having a professional sculptor, either deliberately or by

accident in the carving process, interfere with the function the figure is to perform. For this reason, Dahomean wood sculptures vary considerably in quality.

These figures are compact in design and heavy in forms that express mass. Many have a disproportionately short body and long legs and a moderately large head that is characteristically round. The surfaces are rugged and without refinement, and the only details are the roughly carved heavy features of the face. A resemblance to the Yoruba style to the east is frequently observable in the oval eyes and heavy lips, while the head shape is comparable to that of Ashanti figures. Dahomean wood sculpture also includes the decoration of a number of utilitarian and ritual objects, such as cups and containers, ax handles, stools, and mortars. On them geometric, human, or sometimes animal forms are carved, either in the round or in relief.

The two important graphic arts of the Dahomeans are the incising of calabashes and appliquéing on cloth. Calabashes are decorated with geometric and stylized plant forms that record proverbs and are largely used to send love offerings from men to women. They are greatly esteemed as possessions, and despite their minor significance they are carved with care. The more spectacular appliqued cloths are made only by members of a restricted family guild living in the city of Abomey. Human and animal forms, usually representing narrative and genre scenes, are arranged in a perspectiveless design that reads from bottom to top. European trade materials of brilliant colors are now used both for the figures that are cut from patterns and for the backgrounds to which they are sewed. The cloth is sold to anyone who can afford it and it is used in many ways, such as for wall hangings, covers for state umbrellas, and for making the caps worn by chiefs. The designs have a rather close stylistic relationship to the clay reliefs.

In many respects the art of Dahomey reveals a tradition that appears to be a composite of several other styles. The naturalism of the small brass figures, for example, suggests a like quality in the Ashanti gold weights, but their finely chased surface designs point to the style of Benin to the southeast. Stylistic analogies with both Ashanti and Yoruba have been pointed out in Dahomean wood carvings, while the use in several media of a genre or narrative subject matter strengthens this analogy. However apparent these similarities with other traditions may be, style elements that are characteristically Dahomean are combined with them to produce a distinctive art.

EAST GUINEA COAST Situated within the political limits of eastern Dahomey and southwestern Nigeria, the East Guinea Coast art area includes the most populous region of native Africa. Three important styles were developed here, those of Yoruba, Benin, and Ife. The art of both Benin and Ife may be considered "ancient" and that of Yoruba "recent."

Among the numerous Yoruban tribes a truly great center of wood carving flourished and still exists to a limited extent today. A distinguishing feature of this style is the extensive use of color. Nowhere else in Negro Africa does color play such a continously important role as it does in their art. The pigments are bright and include a wide range of tones of red, yellow, blue, black, and white. These are combined in many ways to produce an effect of striking polychromy. Their sculpture is also often very large in size.

Numerous carved figures and ritual objects are required in the many rites honoring the nature deities in the vast pantheon of Yoruba gods. Bowls and trays are elaborately sculptured for use in divination rites that have religious sanction and are the particular province of the god Ifa (Pl. 36). A seated female figure with a child at her breast represents the goddess Odudua. This deity has a quasi-historical significance, for Odudua, a man, was reputedly the founder of the Yoruba state. At his death he was deified and became associated with the earth goddess of the same name. In like manner, Shango, a Yoruba king, became at his death the god of thunder, lightning, and storms. He is represented or symbolized variously in sculpture as an armed horseman (Pl. 32), by staffs carved with a double-ax motif, and as female attendant figures. A number of other gods are also represented by carved male or female figures.

Twins in Yoruba are considered sacred. They are pro-

tected by a special god, at whose temples the parents perform the requisite rites. If one of the twins should die, the
parents have a pair of small figures carved (Pl. 33). One of
them is hidden away, and the other serves to replace the
dead child. It is bathed, clothed, and offered food whenever
the surviving child is bathed, clothed, and fed. This is done
by the mother until the survivor is old enough to take care
of the figure in like manner. After the death of the surviving
twin, the carving is carefully preserved for a generation
or so.

The Yoruba use many masks in their men's religious and
social societies. There are two principal types: a nearly life-
size mask worn on the top of the head (Pls. 37, 38), and a
very large, heavy helmet type that fits over the head and
rests on the shoulders (Pl. 39). Both types are often complex
and elaborate in design, human features frequently are
combined with animal, snake, or geometric forms, and figures are arranged in groups on top of the mask. The entire
form, regardless of its complexity of design, is carved from
a single piece of wood. All the masks are brilliantly polychromed. The majority of them are used in funerary rites
for the members of the various societies.

Yoruban sculpture evidences a strong tradition (Pls. 32–
39). Its outstanding element is a vigorous expressive naturalism that is contained within an emphatic sculptural
style. Forms are clearly defined, ample in scale, and are pro-
portioned to lead the eye to a large head. The shapes defining the forms are strongly marked, often roughly carved,
and are essentially naturalistic. Mass and volume are almost
equally emphasized, and carved surface details, always present, are sometimes elaborately painted. Facial features are
large in scale, particularly the eyes, which are often large
painted ovals. In the majority of examples all detail is
carved in low relief, rather than incised on the surface.
Primarily characteristic of Yoruba style are polychromy,
grouping of forms into compositions, and vigorous expressive naturalism. A wide variety of poses reflect many aspects
of the life of these people.

The art of the old kingdom of Benin belongs to the same
basic tradition as that of the Yoruba. It consists of a great

number of bronze ritual objects and insignia of rank that were cast in the round or in relief by the cire-perdue process. The finest examples represent a technical excellence unsurpassed in this medium by any country or era. A number of objects of outstanding quality were also carved in ivory. But the preferred African medium of wood carving is represented by only a few comparatively recent examples that are inferior both in technique and in style.

Benin sculpture is unique in several respects. It is the only African Negro art with any semblance of chronological sequence and with a complex iconography. The forms and symbols that occur in this sculpture largely refer to the "oba" (king), either as a deified spiritual and political leader, or in his guise as "Olokun," god of the sea. In no other Negro African kingdom was the concept of absolutism and divinity of the king more fully developed. During and after his lifetime the power and importance of the oba was supreme. A state religion centered around the annual commemorative and propitiatory rites to the ancestral obas. In these rites the majority of the bronzes were used, and at them human sacrifices, the prerogative of royalty, were made. Benin art is therefore largely a royal art, ancestral in character and religious and political in meaning.

The kingdom of Benin was discovered by the Portuguese in 1472. With the exception of an eighteenth- to nineteenth-century interregnum, commercial and missionary contacts with Europe have persisted from that date to the present time. But in spite of these contacts and the detailed accounts of the magnificence of Benin City by Dutch travelers in the seventeenth century, the art of this great African kingdom was little known until the end of the nineteenth century. In 1897, as the result of an unfortunate incident, the British sent a punitive expedition against Benin, and during the course of the fighting the city was burned. As a result of the fire, several thousand bronze figures and reliefs that had been hidden away during civil wars in the eighteenth century were discovered.

It was at first believed that these highly accomplished bronzes were the result of Portuguese contacts in the fifteenth century; but it was subsequently recognized that the reliefs depicting Portuguese soldiers were stylistically and technically too developed to represent early works in a new and difficult medium. On the basis of this recognition hypothetical chronologies were proposed for these bronzes.[4] The early period by these calculations is the thirteenth century, the period of highest achievement the late sixteenth and early seventeenth centuries, and a period of decadence from the seventeenth into the eighteenth century. This chronology is at least in part corroborated by a Benin tradition, which states that bronze casting was introduced in the thirteenth century. It is now generally agreed that the technique of cire-perdue casting was established long before the Portuguese arrived in Benin, but that the Portuguese by their importation of brass made the metal readily available and so facilitated the development of the art.

Relief plaques (Pl. 42) representing the king, royal retainers, and genre scenes were apparently made, according to Dutch seventeenth-century accounts, to decorate the façades of the structures along the wide central avenue of Benin City. The figures depicted are modeled in high relief, and details of costume and accoutrements are fully described. In almost every case the figures are set against a background richly decorated with large chased four-leaf designs and a pitted surface. Many bronze ritual objects, such as scepters, staffs, gongs, and bells (Pl. 43), are also elaborately decorated with modeled and chased surface designs.

The majority of ritual objects were made for use on the royal altars, where the oba offered periodic sacrifices to his ancestors. The altars contained animal figures and groups of human figures in the round and, most important of all, a number of bronze heads (Pl. 41). Three types of head were used. Two of them are almost life size, one, with a high pointed headdress, presumably representing a female, and the other, with a close fitting rounded head-gear, a male. The third type is much larger than life size and represents the oba (Pl. 41). Huge elephant tusks were fitted into the

[4] Cf. Luschan, Die Altertümer von Benin, Berlin, 1919, 3 vols. Struck, Die Chronologie der Benin-Altertümer, *Zeitschrift für Ethnologie*, LV (1923), 113–166.

open top of the large heads and were at least partially supported by the vertical, wing-like forms on the heads. Both
the large bronze heads and the tusks were entirely the pre-
rogatives of the oba. The tusks were completely carved in
relief with representations and symbols of the oba in his
dual role as king and deity.

Comparatively few Benin ivories have survived. Female
statuettes (Pl. 44) were carved in this medium, and small
chalice-like cups were carefully decorated with relief and
pierced designs. A number of large bracelets or armlets,
sculptured in ivory or cast in bronze, were also decorated
with intricate openwork designs.

Benin style emphasizes the elements characteristic of the
art of the East Guinea Coast area—heaviness of shape, squat-
ness of form, and disproportionate largeness of head. Distinctive of Benin art, however, are profuseness of descriptive detail and full, expansive volumes. These qualities
give the sculpture a definiteness of iconography and a monu-
mental scale that is unparalleled in African Negro art. A
good deal of the iconography, or meaning of the elaborate
detail, has been interpreted, and the greater part of it refers
to the political or religious role of the oba. Benin art is
based, perhaps more than is that of any other African style
or tradition, on reality; the details of figures and costumes
represent actual ceremonial dress, and the persons and animals, those participating in the rites. Technically, the quality of the cire-perdue casting and the magnificently chased
surfaces of Benin bronzes of the best period are unexcelled
by those of the Italian Renaissance or of the Far East. However, the sharpness and preciseness of line and of edges,
found also in Yoruba wood carving, suggests that elements
of this style may possibly have originated in the medium of
a hard, resistant material, such as ivory.

The now-famous Ife bronze and terra cotta heads also
come from this part of Nigeria. But they stand apart and
apparently do not belong to any Negro African style tradition. In both media a penetrating naturalism characterizes
the superbly modeled heads (Pl. 40). A strong plastic construction is achieved by very sensitive and adroitly modeled
surface planes that define with complete sureness both the

bony structure and the fleshy parts. Unlike any other African Negro sculptural style, these heads have an absolute naturalism of proportion and of facial features. Each example, moreover, is individualized so definitely that these heads must be recognized as portraits. In both bronze and terra cotta, the finest specimens reveal a perfected and refined technique.

A Benin tradition states that the art of bronze casting was acquired from Ife about 1280. Stylistically, however, there is little similarity between the sculpture of Benin and Ife.

Frobenius, who in 1910 publicized his discovery of several Ife terra cotta heads and one bronze head, believed that they were Mediterranean, possibly Etruscan in style; while the Egyptologist Petrie found them very close to Memphite work of the fifth century B.C. Since that time, a number of heads have been discovered at Ife.[5] It seems evident that the city had been for a very long time a holy city, both for the Yoruba tribes to the north and for Benin. The heads may therefore have been portraits of important religious leaders. In support of this, the majority of the heads were still considered sacred when they were discovered and were set up within the precincts of a sacred grove.

There is little doubt that the strong characterization and technical excellence of the Ife terra cotta and bronze heads represent the high point of a long tradition. But how a tradition so unlike those of Negro Africa in its complete naturalism came to be developed in this area must remain for the moment pure speculation. It seems likely, however, that if the art of bronze casting had been introduced into Benin from Ife at a time when the finely modeled portraits were being made at Ife some evidence of the Ife style would be perceptible in the early Benin bronzes. The absence of that evidence suggests either that the art of Ife had not reached that high level of development by the late thirteenth century or that it had passed it and the style had become degenerate. Future systematic archaeological investigations may reveal the answer to the present enigma of Ife art. But until

[5] Cf. Bascom, "Brass Portrait Heads from Ile-Ife, Nigeria," *Man,* XXXVIII (1938), 176; Eva H. and V. Meyerowitz, Bronzes and Terra-Cottas from Ile-Ife," *Burlington Magazine,* LXXV (1939), 150–155.

that time, it must remain unique and apart from other African Negro styles.

NIGER RIVER DELTA East of the lower reaches of the Niger River, and in what is now southeastern Nigeria, the sculpture of the Ibo, Ibibio, Ijaw, and Ekoi tribes represent another distinct tradition. The region is occupied by many subtribes and the cultural elements are diverse. Each of the four major groups of tribes has developed an art that is distinguished by certain style characteristics; but the style of each tribe contains a number of elements common to the entire area.

A marked feature of Niger Delta sculpture is its use of naturalistic and abstract forms. Bold geometric shapes often appear in the composition of these forms, and there is a conspicuous absence of surface decoration and descriptive detail. The carvings are frequently painted, although the range of colors is limited to red, white, black, and yellow, and the intensity of tones is far below that of Yoruba work. Dramatic expression is emphasized, and shapes, designs, and colors are used towards this end.

The sculpture of this area is largely carved in wood, although clay modeled figures are extensively made by several tribes. A great number and variety of masks are carved, the majority of them based on an abstraction of human forms, others on animal or bird heads. All the principal types of African masks are found in this area—the face and helmet types and that worn or carried on the head. Many of them are life-size; others are very large. A quantity of small human figures are also carved in wood. The styles of these figures vary in details from tribe to tribe, but they are all generic rather than individualized in treatment. Ritual objects, such as drums, stools, and staffs, are frequently decorated with geometric or figure designs.

Throughout this area ancestor worship is the dominant religious belief. Figures, masks, and ceremonial objects are used in the rites motivated by this belief. Personalized nature spirits, showing volition and intent, are also represented in this art. In many regions they are considered important but minor spirits in an organized pantheon headed by the major deities that personify natural forces. Rites and portions of ceremonies with magical intent are common, and in many instances an indwelling or impersonal force is believed to reside in the carving and to be a source of power. Figures and masks are employed in a great many rites. In many cases they symbolize the spirit, deity, or ancestor and do not represent it or serve as a temporary abode for it.

Secret societies are conspicuous features of the culture of the Niger Delta area. Some are basically religious in purpose, and their rites are performed in honor of their ancestors or of the spirits or deities who serve as their tutelary gods. Other secret societies are social, political, or economic. As in other parts of Africa, masks are used by these secret societies. Distinctive of this area, however, is the performance by the secret societies of one or more "plays" that it alone owns. Marionettes, carved as small wooden human figures, are used in these "plays," which seem to have magical and symbolic significance.

The Ibo are the most numerous and the most northerly of the Niger Delta tribes. Their art consists of many wooden masks, a unique type of symbolic power figure, and many singular clay-modeled figures. The masks are used by the Maw secret society in their funerary rites and are the best known of Ibo sculptures. They are carefully carved and are based expressively on the human skull (Pls. 45, 46). The eyes, for example, suggest round, empty eye sockets. The face is narrow and emaciated, and the teeth are carved exposed, as though the flesh around them had disappeared. A thin white paint, symbolic of the spirit content of the masks, covers the face, while the elaborately varied and often crested hairdress is painted black and the skeletal eye sockets and mouth red. It is believed that during some of the mortuary ceremonies the ancestors speak through these masks. They are characterized by a thinness and delicacy of surface planes and by their dramatic power.

Ibo figure sculpture, as it appears in the power carvings, is more interesting for its symbolism and the openness of its design than for its aesthetic quality. This type of carving, known as Ikengga, usually consists of a seated figure supporting on its head a variety of forms that symbolize such commendable virtues as strength, courage, and virility. These sculptures have no ostensible religious meaning and may be purchased in the open market by a father for his son. They symbolize the qualities the father wishes the boy to develop, and they are set up within the home where the boy can make constant offerings to them. It seems that eventually these carvings assume the role of talismans for the boy. The figures are composed of thick-set forms, and the symbolic shapes at the top are essentially descriptive.

Far more interesting ethnologically and aesthetically are the polychromed clay figures that represent deities and genre subjects and are made for use in the religious rites connected with the construction and dedication of the Mbari temples. These structures are built and decorated by a specially selected group for the purpose of honoring various gods of the Ibo pantheon. Many of the clay figures, modeled on light palm-wood armatures, are larger than life-size, and they have similar proportions and details. The torsos are long, slender columns, the arms and legs are very short, often flexed in an animated pose, and the head surmounts a long thick neck. Facial features are small in scale and are placed well below the high arched eyebrows. The basic color is white, and the details are rendered in various shades of red, brown, and black. These highly stylized figures have a verve and a dramatic character that is common to all Niger Delta styles.

The art of the Ibibio tribes who live south of the Ibo includes various types of masks and both large and small wooden figures. Many Ibibio masks are used in secret society rites; the most distinctive type is that carried on or held above the head. Some of these consist of one or two seated figures that are two or three feet high (Pl. 47), others of groups of five or six small figures. In many of the masks the human figure is combined with geometric forms. The majority of Ibibio masks are of the monoxyle type, that is, they are carved from a single piece of wood; but some of them are composite, or are composed of several separately carved parts. Ibibio masks of all types are often painted a

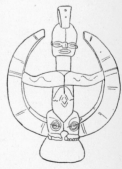

monochrome, dull black; others, however, are painted in
colors similar to those used by the Ibo.

Both masks and carved figures are used by the Ibibio in
their secret society rites, many of them of the "play"
variety. Some of the small figures symbolize the presence
or the participation of ancestors in the rites, others the
minor or tutelary deities of the society. The carved figures
are also often set up during the rites in a prescribed order,
or are carried in processions. Sacrifices of human beings are
frequently made to these carved figures. They range in size
from eight inches to life size; some are painted a dull black;
others, white, red, and black. The secret society rites in
which these figures and masks are used are frequently directed to the ancestors from whom certain benefits, such as
fertility of crops and humans, benefits from trade, and good
health are to be had. Some of the smaller figures are also
used in ancestral rites that are independent of those of the
secret societies.

Ibibio style, whether in masks or figures, is marked by
boldness and vigor. The figure, for example, is often described by simplified, geometric shapes. They are always
articulated and clearly marked off from one another, and
they are also integrated so that the totality of the form is
emphasized. Surface refinement and a precise delineation
of detail is foreign to this style. Volume, mass, and detail is
suggested rather than defined, and in this way vitality and
vigor are emphasized.

In comparison with Ibo art, that of the Ibibio has greater
boldness of form and expression. There are, however, many
similarities in the forms and in the designs of the figures
and masks of these two tribes.

The Ijaw tribes, who live in the heart of the Niger Delta
country, have developed one of the most distinctive styles
of this area. It is composed of strictly geometric forms,
roughness of technique, and dramatic aggressiveness of expression. Ijaw figures, whether small or life size, are symbols
of deities, spirits, and ancestors. Flat, plank-like forms represent the body, while the somewhat more rounded arms
and legs are carved as though attached to the body, but not
integrated with it. The head is oval, the forehead rounded

and projecting, and the face a flat surface with the eyes and
oval mouth protruding. Teeth are prominently carved in
the oval mouth, giving the figure a menacing expression.

Ijaw figures are set up in shrines in honor of the ancestors
of the chief. These consist of separately carved figures of the
chief and members of his family which are attached to a
solid background of horizontal rods. The entire screen-like
background is framed at the sides and top by wide boards.
Heads of additional ancestors are carved in the round and
placed along the top of the frame. Such screens range from
four to six feet high.

Ijaw masks are usually of the type worn or carried on the
head. They are often remarkable for their aesthetically bold
and striking geometric designs. Animals and fish frequently
form the basis for these masks, but human heads and features are also used, the latter resembling the heads of the
figures on the screens, although more dramatically developed (Pls. 48, 49). Some of these masks and some of the
figures are used in secret society "plays" that are associated
with fertility, burial, and war ceremonies.

The Ekoi tribes in the extreme eastern part of the Niger
Delta area have created a unique type of mask. It consists
in most cases of a human head (Pl. 50), frequently a janus
type, that is carved in wood and covered with rigidly
stretched skin. These masks, like many made by the Ijaw,
are worn on top of the head, usually in funerary rites, and
represent deceased ancestors. In the past human skin was
used to cover these carvings, but recently monkey and antelope skins have been used. In this type of mask all details
are first carved on the wooden frame and then the skin is
pressed tightly over the carved surface. Some examples
show that a poker technique was used, that is, a hot iron or
piece of metal was employed to press the skin into the
carved wooden design. The expression of these masks is aggressive and naturalistic. The mouth, for example, is open,
and the teeth, sometimes represented by metal inlay, give a
fierce expression. The bony structure of the head and the
face is often lucidly defined. Although unique in many
respects, the Ekoi figure and mask style has a number of
elements in common with other Niger Delta styles.

III CAMEROON

EAST AND SOUTHEAST of the Niger Delta area a significant art tradition is represented by the sculptures of a number of small tribes living within the borders of the present political province of Cameroon. Although several substyles may be distinguished, the art of the Cameroon area represents one of the most homogeneous styles in Negro Africa. Wood carvings that include large house posts, masks, and ritual objects are sculptured with an intensive, alert expression. Carved shapes emphasize dramatic forms that express movement. Refinement of surfaces is unknown. A rough technique utilizes human and animal forms to create dramatic, often large-scale dynamic volumes. Angular rhythmic patterns of shapes and lines are common to the Cameroon style. Similar qualities appear in smaller pottery vessels and in pottery and brass pipe bowls and staffs. It is a distinctive and a very strong style.

The tribes that produce this art live in the high inland plateau known as the Grasslands.[1] They are basically an agricultural people who have similar cultural backgrounds. The existence among these tribes of numerous graded and totemic secret societies is of particular importance for their art. Masks, figures, and other ritual sculptures are required for use in the many ceremonies of these societies. A considerable amount of secular art of social or prestige significance is also typical of this area. Large carved wooden door frames and supporting posts, for example, are frequently used to decorate the house of a chief. Pipes, with their bowls elaborately modeled in clay or cast in brass, are also used by those of high rank. In some regions, stools and low wooden beds are carved for use by the same class. Red, blue, white,

[1] The most important of these tribes are the Bamum, Bangwa, Bafum, Bafo, Bamenda, and Bali.

and black beads are used in many cases to cover wooden stools, long-necked calabash vessels, and ceremonial wearing apparel. A great number of masks are used in the Cameroons in both secret and public rites.

Figure sculpture in the Cameroon area ranges from very small to almost life-size carvings. Poses are frequently contorted to express movement, and the rigid axis so usual in many other African styles is therefore conspicuously absent (Pls. 51, 53–54). Proportions vary considerably. In some figures they are short, heavy, and close-knit, and in others, elongated, thin, and rather loosely composed. Regardless of proportions, the shapes of the figures are full volumed and emphatically defined, frequently by the device of constricting areas at the points of articulation. But the shapes are well integrated and rhythmically related, and in some instances they have a marked cubistic appearance. The figures are usually painted a dull red monochrome; sometimes they were stained a dull black or left entirely unpainted, while a few examples show that white was at times used to emphasize facial features. In some cases the figures are covered with beads, usually in the three preferred colors of red, black, and white.

The considerable number of human figures carved in Cameroon are occasioned by the demands of the many graded secret societies. In the rites of these societies the figure serves as a temporary residing place for ancestral spirits. Human figures are also used as architectual carvings. Short or tall supporting posts, either attached to the wall surface or free standing, are frequently carved with a number of small superposed figures. A similar type of carving is often used on large door frames.

Many Cameroon stools are carved with human or animal figures as functional supports (Pl. 56). There are two principal types of sculptured stools: one has a solid central supporting stem of lesser diameter than that of the circular top and bottom, and the other, usually larger, has a hollow cylindrical support with a solid circular top. One or more human or animal figures are often carved as supports in the stem type, and a number of figures, usually arranged in two tiers, in the cylindrical. These stools represent the highest achievement of Cameroon sculptural design. Within a composition of two or more figures, a few major motives are organized by the use of accented variations, such as alternation, inversion, and transposition of the main theme. A rhythmic pattern is composed of the free spaces surrounding the forms and of the arrangement of volumes, masses, and lines within the design.

A great number of masks of exceptionally strong aesthetic quality are carved in this area. These vary considerably in size, design, and meaning. Three kinds of masks may be distinguished: a life-sized representation of human features, a very large mask that combines human and animal forms, and a smaller realistic animal type. A rhythmic arrangement of large-scale features is apparent in all these masks. The mouth is frequently open to achieve the desired dramatic expressiveness. Color is used sparingly. The majority of masks are either unpainted or are stained a dull black or earth-red monochrome. Some of the animal masks, however, are slightly polychromed, often being painted with earth red, light green, black, and white. The dramatic expressiveness of these masks is comparable to the animated pose and vigor of form of Cameroon figure sculpture.

The naturalistic human type of mask is used by the religious and military secret societies, while the larger and more spectacular masks are worn in the rites of the totemic secret societies. These societies are composed of groups of individuals, independent of tribe or family, who have animals as protectors or as sources of power. In some cases membership is hereditary, but it is usually the result of circumstances or accomplishments. The masks represent the protective or power animal. They are usually worn at a sharp angle on top of the head. The animals most freqently represented by these masks are the chimpanzee, the elephant, the buffalo, and the antelope.

Animals are more important in Cameroon art than in that of most other African areas. The antelope, for example, appears in many of the cylindrical-type stools, and monkey and snake forms on the stem-type stools. Lizards and monkeys are also used in combination with human forms in many of the architectural carvings. Animals have the animation and the dramatic expressiveness depicted in the human forms.

Cameroon art also includes many decorative ritual and utilitarian objects, such as ceremonial vessels of urn shape, pipe bowls, staff heads, and small votive figures. They are carved in wood, modeled in clay, or cast in brass. Numerous vessels are sculptured in wood, either as free-standing forms supported by a stem or as bowls held by carved human or animal figures (Pl. 52, 55). Other vessels are modeled in clay and are decorated with human, animal, or geometric forms in relief or, in some cases, partially in the round. These are not glazed, but have a dull dark red, gray, or black color. A number of pipe bowls are also modeled in clay and represent human, semi-human, or fantastic figures (Pl. 62); others are cast in brass and depict human mask-like heads or figures and animal heads. Brass casting is an important Cameroon art, and many staff heads, usually modeled as short, compact figures, together with pipe bowls, best represent this metal art (Pl. 61). A pierced, geometric lattice-like detail is often used on the brass staff heads and the pipe bowls. Small human and animal masks are also modeled in clay and cast in brass (Pl. 60).

The style tradition manifested in Cameroon art is vigorous and strong. In its dramatic quality and expression of movement it is comparable to the Niger Delta style, while the sharp delineation of facial features and in some cases the shape and scale of these features are somewhat analogous to elements of Benin and Yoruba style. It is, however, one of the most vital and homogeneous of all African Negro styles.

IV CENTRAL AFRICA

THE ENTIRE vast sculpture-producing area of Central Africa is peopled with few exceptions by Bantu-speaking Negroes. But the social and political structure of their culture is similar to that of West Africa, and they, too, depend economically upon agriculture. Central African villages, however, are smaller, and there is in this region even greater evidence of intermingling of tribes and diffusion of cultural elements. Seven clearly defined traditions can be distinguished in this Central African area. Most of them are related more closely on a stylistic basis with one another than are the West African traditions.

NORTHWEST AREA   A strong art tradition is evident in the northwestern part of this region, embracing the political limits of southeastern Cameroon and of Gabun and Spanish Guinea. Three distinctive, but related, styles represent this tradition: that of the Fang tribes in the north, of the Bakota in the central portion, and of the tribes in the Ogowe River region towards the south. The art of the entire area lacks the variety of forms and types and the dramatic expression of movement characteristic of Cameroon sculpture. Among the Fang the human figure, half-figure, or head predominate, and little other sculpture is found. Bakota art is almost entirely restricted to highly stylized metal figures; while the Ogowe River style is expressed only in masks that show little variety. No masks were used by the Fang tribes or by the Bakota, and no figures by the Ogowe River people.

The style of the Northwest area is based on fluid curves, decorative patterns, and subtle contrasts. A refinement of detail and surface unknown in the vigorous, dramatic Cameroon art are basic elements in the sculpture of this

tradition. Figures and masks are, with few exceptions, associated with or function as containers of the spirits of the
dead. It is evident, therefore, that a strong ancestor cult
prevails in this area. Among the Fang and the Bakota in the
northern part of this region the art is connected directly
with ancestor rites, while to the south, in the Ogowe River
region, it is associated with the ancestors or ancestral spirits
of secret societies. Figures, half-figures, and heads are also
used, particularly among the Fang tribes, as decorations for
their stringed musical instruments, drums, and spoons.

Fang sculpture is the work of a number of related tribes
who live in the southern part of Cameroon, in Spanish
Guinea, and in northern Gabun. They are war-like, canni-
balistic tribes who invaded this region and became over-
lords of the weaker indigenous peoples whom they conquered. It is believed that they came from the northeast,
from the upper Ubangi River area, since they have certain
cultural elements in common with the Azandeh, who live
there. Fang art, sometimes designated by the tribal names
Pangwe and Pahouin, includes a limited number of forms.
These are male or female full figures, half-figures, and heads
that are carved as free standing or are used decoratively on
musical instruments or a few utilitarian objects. The essen-
tials of this style are similar, although the details vary from
tribe to tribe. For example, the sculpture of the Fang tribes
who live in the Cameroon region evidences some of the
dramatic aggressiveness of Cameroon style, while that to
the south expresses a quiet aloofness.

Fang art is best typified by its well-known mortuary
carvings. These include full figures, half-figures, and heads
that are attached to the sides of cylindrical bark boxes in
which ancestral skulls are placed. It is believed that strong
spirits inhabit the sculptures and that they protect the
skulls. At regular intervals the ancestral skulls are removed
from the containers, cleaned, and ceremonially anointed
with magical materials that reactivates them. The carvings
are at the same time removed from the boxes, used in
puppet-like fashion in certain rites, cleaned, and rubbed
with materials that insures the continuance of their spirit
power. It is thought that the heads are the oldest of these

Fang sculptures; the half-figures, the second oldest; and the full figures the most recent. This chronological order is supported by the fact that at the time of European contact the heads and half-figures were no longer being used and little was known about them. The styles of the three types are, however, essentially similar.

Fang style consists of emphatically articulated rounded and oval shapes of geometric character (Pls. 63–66). The planes that define these shapes are smooth and refined and permit an easy flow of surface movement. The design relies entirely on a subtle rhythmical harmony of shapes and surfaces, without any carved descriptive or decorative detail whatsoever. Body forms are cylindrical, often elongated, and are conspicuously separated one from the other. The heads are either oval or eliptical, and the facial area is slightly concave, eyes, nose, and mouth carved in relief within the sunken area so as to emphasize the change of surface movement. The smoothness and fluidity of these planes create a sense of contained space within and around the figure, while, in contrast, the projections expand the spacial envelope. Both varieties of spacial form are harmoniously integrated. Fang figures have a quiet aloofness of expression that is at times combined with an aggressive open mouth; potential energy is represented in the schematic organization of their stylized shapes. The figures are painted dull black, dark red, or gray monochrome, although on a few two colors were used, and on some the eyes are inlaid with metal. Many elements in the style of these figures suggest Baoulé figures and masks.

Bakota sculpture to the south differs radically from that of the Fang. Their metal covered ancestral figures represent, in fact, a unique African style (Pls. 69–70). In these, three-dimensional forms flatten out as essentially two-dimensional surfaces. The forms are first shaped in wood and then are covered with sheets or strips of brass or copper. Two-dimensional surfaces, described by flat or slightly concave or convex planes, are arranged in a shallow parallel alignment. The oval shape of the head and the design of facial features are comparable to the design of like elements in Fang style. In Picasso-like fashion, the hair and the back of the head are represented by a crescentric-shape above the face and by wing-like projections set in the same plane at each side. A long cylindrical neck supports the head and is in turn supported by a hollow roughly diamond-shape frame parallel to the forms above. This diamond design is the conventionalization of either a full-length or a half-length figure.

Bakota figures, like those of the Fang, are placed in boxes containing ancestral bones and skulls. These figures are of two sizes—one considerably smaller than the other. Knobs and short spirals project from the heads of the smaller ones which probably represent females, while the larger ones, without such fussy details, may represent males.

Three types of Bakota sculpture may be characterized on the basis of the treatment of the face. In one type the entire area of the face is concave (Pl. 69); in the second, the forehead is a rounded convex surface and the face below convex (Pl. 70). In the third type the forehead is convex and one or more horizontal convex zones cross the concave surface of the face below. The first or concave type is further distinguished by a geometric treatment of the surface. Within the oval of the face a cross is transcribed by bisecting a wide central vertical band by an equally wide central horizontal band. The oval area of the face is therefore divided by the arms of the cross into quadrants. In many examples these quadrants are surfaced with thin strips of copper laid diagonally, thus producing a rich linear design (Pl. 69). The concave type of face is used in both large and small figures, but it is more frequently found in the smaller examples. In the majority of Bakota figures a punched or hammered thin decorative border usually appears around the geometric forms that describe the head.

Although these metal-covered sculptures are characteristic of this tribe, some few wood carvings were made by them. They combine in a very interesting way the highly stylized geometric forms of the Bakota with the three-dimensionality of Fang figures. The result is an angular blocklike figure that is transitional between the styles of these two tribes and makes very clear their association within the same art tradition.

The third style of the Northwest Central African area is represented by the masks of the Ogowe River region. They consist of two groups: those used by the female and those by the male secret societies. Both groups show a preference for rounded and oval shapes and for smooth-flowing surface planes that relate this style to the other two styles of this area. In some masks elaborate surface details, particularly in the rendering of the coiffure, is analogous to the decorative surface patterns found on many of the Bakota metal figures. Ogowe River masks, however, are frequently painted in three colors, red, black, and white, in contrast to the monochrome coloration of the Fang figures and the slight color contrasts between brass and copper in Bakota sculptures.

The most representative Ogowe River masks are those used by the leaders of the female secret society to depict ancestral and guardian spirits (Pls. 71–72). Distinctive of these masks are the carefully carved hairdresses, often arranged in crest-like shape over the top of the head with two pendant forms at the sides. Slanting, oriental-like eyes are also often found, together with the presence of scarification marks carved in high relief and arranged in clusters above the bridge of the nose and at each side of the eyes. The structural and fleshy forms of the face are carved with marked sensitivity and naturalism. Facial areas are usually painted white, the hairdress black, lips red, and when scarification marks appear they are painted black. Surfaces are smoothly and evenly carved, details sharply and cleanly defined, and the paint rather thinly applied. The majority of female masks are fairly small and have a band of rough carving around the carefully finished forms and surfaces which is covered when the masks are worn by a surrounding ₁affia fringe. In technique and expression, they are among the most sensitive of Negro masks.

A greater variety is found in the male secret society masks of this area. Some are rectangular, others are wide ovals; but all of them have a concave facial surface analogous to Fang and Bakota figures. They differ strikingly from the female masks in many important respects. For example, they are restricted entirely to a representation of the facial area, and no hairdress is indicated. Scarification marks and other high-relief designs are absent, although some have an incised pattern that may represent face painting. The naturalistic and descriptive treatment of structure and detail such as are characteristic of the female masks are not found on these male masks, but there is a marked fluidity of surface planes and a refinement of carving that establishes a stylistic tie with the female Ogowe River masks and with the Fang and Bakota sculptures.

The male masks, like the female ones, are worn by leaders of the secret society and also represent strong protective ancestral spirits. Some were used in mortuary rites and others in initiation ceremonies. In some cases the wearer of the mask walked or danced on stilts, his body covered by a long costume that reached to the ground. Color was used more sparingly than on the female masks, the majority of them being painted a white, red, or black monochrome.

The art of the Northwest Central African area represents through its three distinct but related styles a very important Negro African tradition. Refinement of technique and design appear alike in the handling of three-dimensional forms, two-dimensional line patterns, and naturalistic structure. But in all cases a strong pervading unity results from the clearly organized designs and stands out as a characteristic element of this style.

South and east of this area the vast expanse of the Congo-Ubangi River system was, before European explorations and conquests of the past seventy-five years had disrupted the old patterns of life, one of the richest art-producing areas of Africa. In the sculpture from this region a number of important traditions may be discerned. Many of them are at least partly related to one another, with the result that a greater homogeneity appears in the sculpture of this area than elsewhere in Africa. The region, largely contained within the present political limits of the Belgian Congo, is inhabited by a great number of tribes, most of whom speak a variety of dialects of one linguistic stock, the Bantu. In the past the economy was basically agricultural, supplemented here and there by hunting. Although many cultures were developed, there was throughout this large area

considerable diffusion of common cultural elements, such
as initiation rites, fetishism, poison ordeal, and types of art
objects. Many sculptural style elements were also widely
distributed.

The physical environment of this region consists of heavy
forests, especially along the main courses of the rivers, and
comparatively open forests and grasslands. In the more
heavily populated central and southern parts the rivers,
with few exceptions, flow north, emptying into the Congo
or the major branches of the Congo, and divide the land
into a number of parallel north-south compartments. The
most important of these rivers are, from west to east, the
Kwango, the Kwilu, the Kasai, the Sankuru, the Lomami,
and the Lualaba. But neither the forests nor the rivers created insurmountable barriers to communication. A very
considerable shifting of peoples have, in fact, characterized
the entire area. They were largely caused by invasions from
east, south, and north and by intertribal wars. Trade contacts, however, also existed widely. It is not surprising,
therefore, that many cultural elements were common to the
tribes who lived in this extensive area.

The entire south-southeast region of Central Africa
may be designated, irrespective of present political bound-
aries, as the Congo area. Six clearly defined art traditions
can be distinguished in this region. These may be local-
ized from west to east on the basis of the various river
systems. The Lower Congo tradition, for example, extends
from the coast to near the Kwango River, while that of
the Western Congo lies between the Kwango and the
Kwilu rivers. A third art area, the Central Congo, centers
around the Kasai-Sankuru watershed in the heart of the
Congo, and a fourth, the Eastern Congo is contained within
the region between the Lomami River and Lake Tanganyika. Two other traditions were developed over extensive
regions in the Southern and the Northern Congo.

LOWER CONGO   The Lower Congo art style appears most
clearly in a varied group of commemorative ancestor and
fetish figures. The tradition is one of naturalistically posed
figures carved in the round. Full-volumed forms are ar-

ranged in a design that emphasizes structural and rhythmic
relationships. The vigor of forms and poses conveys a monumentality and tenseness of expression.

The highest aesthetic quality in Lower Congo sculpture is achieved in the commemorative ancestor figures (Pls. 73–76). These are carved to honor both male and female ancestors, the figures represented as kneeling or seated in tailor fashion on a plinth. Female ancestors usually hold a child on the lap or to the breast. Proportions in both male and female figures are often more naturalistic than is usual in African sculpture. There is a tendency, however, towards short legs, disproportionately long torsos and arms, and a large, impressive head. The expressiveness of these carvings does not derive from the head alone, but from the figure as a whole. Descriptive details, such as scarification marks, bracelets, armlets, and often the inclusion of carved finger nails, are carefully rendered. Openness of design is distinctive of this style. Large-volumed forms, for example, are carved free and in the round, each existing as a completely realized three-dimensional shape. Structural and rhythmic relationships between them are so emphasized in the design that the entire figure is given a closely integrated unity of volumes, shapes, and line patterns. The design is often remarkable for its interpretation of naturalistic shapes and succeeds in portraying that vitality in rich sculptural terms. Figures are usually posed in an attitude of homage or respect, the torso and neck inclined slightly forward and the large head tilted backward.

In the Lower Congo style, heads are nearly round, faces very wide, and features large in scale. The ovals of the eyes are widely spaced, the noses somewhat short, and the mouth, often half-open to show the filed teeth, is enormous, generally half-circular, having a straight lower lip and a curved upper lip. Shell or glass inlay frequently appears in the eyes, although they are often carved with the upper lid drawn down as though half closed. The hair or hairdress varies considerably. In some examples it is conical, in others a square cap, and sometimes it follows the natural curvature of the head. Deeply incised lines are often used to suggest the hair, but in many cases the surface of the head is smooth and undecorated. A rather heavy cylindrical neck, marking off by a sharp line the head from the body, is characteristic of this style.

Throughout the Lower Congo area, among the Bakongo, Bayombe, and various other tribes, commemorative figures are revered, but not worshiped. They were formerly preserved in the huts of descendants, and in recent times they have been placed on the tomb of the deceased. It is with some justification, therefore, that these sculptures have been compared with our tombstones and grave memorials.

The prevalence of commemorative figures in this region probably represent the survival of a strong ancestor cult that later lost much of its religious significance, but retained a religious sanction and became largely a manifestation of social importance. Thus, each commemorative figure was to a large degree personalized. They are not, however, individualized portraits, but are rather generically carved figure types. For example, scarification marks, hairdress, armbands, and other personal ornaments are clearly carved as both tribal and individual identifying details. The heads of only a few figures have the quality of a sensitively rendered portrait.

An individual characterization in Lower Congo commemorative figures appears largely in the reality of their poses. A person renowned as a musician, for example, is represented as seated and playing a musical instrument. Many women who were both good and successful mothers are shown holding a child to the breast or on their laps.[2]

The most important functional religious carvings of this region are the fetish figures. These vary considerably in size and aesthetic quality. Some are small and as carefully carved as the commemorative figures; others are much larger and are roughly sculptured. The numerous small mother and child fetish figures are particularly important. They resemble in pose and style the commemorative figures, with, however, the addition of a circular protrusion

[2] It is possible that the mother and child figures carved in this area may show the influence of Christian Virgin and Child ideas that were introduced to this coast as early as the sixteenth century by Catholic missionaries. But motherhood was highly esteemed in this and many other Negro African areas long before European contact.

from the center of the abdomen, where the magical material was inserted. It is possible that these maternity fetishes
and their magical significance may also owe something to
the influence of Christian beliefs. Kneeling female fetish
figures of like quality, although usually larger, may likewise
have served as maternity fetishes (Pl. 74).

Many Lower Congo fetish sculptures are of greater ethnological than aesthetic interest. The well-known "konde,"
or nail fetish, belongs to this group. It is often of considerable size and is always less carefully carved than are the figures just described. Konde proportions are heavy, the
shapes roughly defined, and facial features are expressively
aggressive. Magical materials are inserted in the abdomen
and also sometimes in the head. It is believed that the indwelling soul or power of this fetish acts as an intermediary
to terrifying spirits whose province is to spread incurable
diseases and cause violent death. Petitions are directed to
the figure by the fetisher, who knows the necessary procedure and drives nails and pieces of metal into the carving
to secure the attention of its indwelling soul. Konde figures
are public fetishes, and the fetisher associated with them
closely resembles a priest.

A number of small animal carvings are related to the
konde fetishes in content and function. They often represent strange hybrid animals composed of dog and feline
forms.

There are many other types of Lower Congo fetishes. All
of them are believed to be intermediaries with the spirit
world. A number of them are associated with benevolent
spirits who are primarily concerned with the well being of
mankind. Fetishes of this type are usually rather small and
are often used by their owner without benefit of a fetisher
in the privacy of the family hut. But regardlesss of size or
type, the majority of Lower Congo fetishes have magical
materials inserted in the abdominal cavity, often covered
with a piece of mirror or white porcelain. Both of these
materials, of European origin, are also frequently used as
inlays for the eyes. Although fetish figures are usually
roughly carved, the concept of organic structure and the
pose of the torso and head reveal basic style characteristics

similar to those of the commemorative figures and indicate
that both groups embody the same sculptural tradition.
This tradition, represented by the sculpture of the many
tribes of this area, is particularly distinctive for its strong
basis in naturalistic forms.

WESTERN CONGO   To the east of the Lower Congo area the
figures and masks of the Bateke, the Bayaka, and the Bapende tribes represent a tradition of compact stylized forms,
angular rhythms, and an impressive handling of facial features. This tradition may be designated as Western Congo.
It prevails in an area between the Kwango and the Kwilu
rivers which extends northwesterly into the political limits
of the French Congo. The art of this region is also stylistically homogeneous, but is less so and more tribally distinguishable than that of the Lower Congo area.

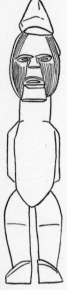

Very small fetish figures averaging about eight inches
high are typical of the Bateke style (Pl. 77). They are full-
length standing figures, usually asexual. They are compact,
the arms never cut free from the body, and the pose is stiff
and frontal. In proportions they differ considerably from
the Lower Congo figures. The legs are short, heavy, and
flexed; the torso is long and columnar; and the very large
head and spool-like neck are together nearly as long as the
torso. The parts of the body, sharply marked off from one
another, have a geometric stylization and are not conceived
as volumes in space, but rather as spacial linear patterns. By
far the greatest attention is devoted to the head, the torso
often being covered with a globular mass of magical material. The head is long and narrow; the coiffure variable,
sometimes crested, sometimes a flat cap-like form; and the
forehead is rounded and protruding. Facial features are
usually composed of narrow, sharp-pointed eyes set close
together, a short, flat nose, a large open oval mouth carved
in high relief, and a short, square-shape beard. Distinctive
scarification marks usually consist of fine parallel incisions
cut on the cheeks from eye to jaw. The sculptural technique
is rough, but vigorous, and remaining knife marks often
give a textural quality to the surfaces. Angular rhythms, the
expression of downward pressing weight, and the sculp-

tural detachment of the large heads are typical of this style.

Bateke fetishes represent one of the distinctive sculptural traditions of the Congo. "Bateke" is a collective term used to designate a number of related tribes who live on both banks of the Congo River and northwestwardly into the French Congo region. Their name signifies that they are traders. They migrated into this area from the south to the southeast, and it seems likely that they brought with them a developed fetishism. Their influence, largely through trade contacts, was widespread over a large area of the western Congo. It appears that the relatively late development of fetishism in this area was at least partly the result of Bateke contacts.

The Bayaka tribes, who live to the south along and to the east of the Kwango River, also carved a number of fetish figures. These resemble those of the Bateke in their design, proportions, and surface treatment. But Bayaka figures are often larger and have more dramatic angularity of pose than those of the Bateke. The greatest differences, however, appear in the treatment of heads and facial features. The head is often shorter than that of Bateke figures and is frequently topped by a crest-like hairdress. Facial features are very large in scale and are spread out over the entire surface of the face below the rounded forehead. Peculiar to Bayaka style are the large tab-like ears that project at right angles from the sides of the head; the very large eyes that are shaped in high relief, like cowrie shells; a long nose, with a depressed bridge that often terminates in an enormous, curved end; and an oval mouth, usually with teeth showing, that is carved in the lower part of the face, frequently with little or no chin beneath. Also typical of this style is the continuation of the hair line around the sides of the face to the nostrils, like a rimmed relief carving. Bayaka figures are sometimes asexual, sometimes male or female. In comparison with those of the Bateke, they are more aggressive and dynamic in expression and are often roughly carved.

Some Bayaka figures are nearly life size and are carved with great care. They are probably commemorative ancestor figures. Many of them have a bird or animal form carved in the round on the top of the head in place of a coiffure, and it seems likely that they commemorated an ancestor who was a famous hunter, an occupation of great importance among the Bayaka. They believed that the abundance of game depended upon the goodwill of the ancestors. Figures of this type, therefore, probably functioned as ancestor figures that were petitioned to secure an abundance of game.

The Bayaka style is also represented by a variety of masks, most of them used in circumcision and initiation rites. These masks fall within the three principal types of Congo masks: the helmet type, that fitted either partially or entirely over the head and rested on the shoulders of the wearer; (Pl. 79) the face mask, that was worn over the face; and a type that was made with a handle by which it was carried and held before the face (Pl. 78). More or less complete costumes of raffia and a variety of other materials were usually worn with these masks, since the identity of the wearer had to be concealed as completely as possible. The masked person in many instances became during the time he was wearing the mask the incarnation of the spirit of the ancestor or mythological being represented or symbolized by the mask, and his conduct was prescribed accordingly. Some masks could not be seen, under penalty of death, by anyone not a member of the society entitled to use them. Others were worn publicly, when all members of a village participated in or witnessed the dances. But the actual meaning and use of many Bayaka masks, as of African masks from other areas, have never been divulged and never will be, since many of them are no longer used and this knowledge is fast disappearing.

The Bayaka helmet type of mask is carved from a single piece of wood (Pl. 79). It is large and is found in almost identical form among the neighboring Bapende tribes. This type is without the characteristic Bayaka hooked nose; the nose is, instead, flat and rather small. The eyes are often narrow slits. Surfaces are carved with great sensitivity and expression, and facial features are cut lightly on the surface so as not to create an impression of heaviness. An animal or human figure in the round is often sculptured just above the forehead. The only important difference between the

Bayaka and Bapende versions of this type of mask is the treatment of the mouth: in the Bayaka masks it is open, showing sharp filed teeth; while in the Bapende it is usually closed. The aggressive mouth of the Bayaka masks is in such contrast with the sensitively carved facial planes that a discordant note is struck. The Bapende helmet masks are without this discord and have an expression of almost delicate sensitivity. But a like aggressiveness is found in the skull-like Bapende circumcision masks and in some of the finely carved Bapende ivory mask-like charms.

The handle-type face mask is distinctive of the Bayaka (Pl. 78). They are small and are carved out of a block of soft wood. The features of the face are deeply recessed within an encircling frame. They are often identical with those of the carved figures, but the nose is usually so grossly exaggerated that the end forms a great hook or loop. The eyes are sometimes represented as closed, a narrow slit separating the upper from the lower lid and providing an aperture through which the dancer using the mask could see. On the top of this type of mask a variety of shapes were attached. They represented figures, animals, huts, and abstract forms that were built up out of bamboo, raffia, and clay. This is, therefore, a composite type of mask. It represents specific mythological and ancestral figures or events, which are of instructional value for the novice. These masks are painted red, white, and black and are unique among African masks.

A third type of Bayaka mask is often a life-size face mask. Some of them, however, are much larger than life size and are not worn, but exhibited on the walls of the circumcision huts. These large masks are stylistically striking for their contrasts of flat surfaces and bulbous or rounded forms. They also have a fixed static quality that is unlike other masks of the Congo area. The smaller face masks resemble facial features of many Bayaka figures.

The third Western Congo style, that of the Bapende tribes, is closely related to the Bayaka in the design of helmet masks. A distinguishing feature, however, is the lack in the Bapende masks of the expressed or the implied aggressiveness of the Bayaka ones. In many examples Bapende masks reveal a more fluid surface treatment, a more balanced arrangement of formal elements. The clarity of shapes and definition of forms in Bapende masks further mark them off from Bayaka examples.

Entirely characteristic of Bapende style are the small ivory maskettes. These are used as charms. They vary considerably in design and in quality of style. In the flow of their surface planes, they are comparable to the better examples of the helmet type Bapende and Bayaka masks.

Of the three tribal styles of the Western Congo, those of the Bayaka and the Bapende represent such a fusion of elements that the two actually belong to a single basic tradition. Perhaps the more dramatic and aggressive elements came from the Bayaka and the sensitivity of form and expression from the Bapende. Bateke style also has numerous elements in common with that of the Bayaka and the Bapende, and the three clearly fall within the same tradition.

CENTRAL CONGO   The art of the vast Central Congo area is the result of a fusion of many tribal styles. This region is bordered on the north by the Sankuru River and includes much of the territory drained by the Kasai-Sankuru river system extending eastward as far as the Lualaba River. The area is peopled by a great number of tribes. But the art is best represented by the sculptures of those tribes who were confederated into the Bushongo kingdom. They occupied the heart of the Kasai-Sankuru region. However, the Bakete and the Bapende tribes in the southwestern part of the central portion of this area created a distinctive mask style, while to the east and southeast the Bena Lulua and Basonge tribes carved characteristic masks and figures. Nevertheless, the superb craftsmanship of the Bushongo artist and the wide distribution of his influences as they appear in the richly decorative art on boxes, cups, drums, and various other objects are typical of this area. The productivity of the Central Congo artist was very great. This is reflected by the numerous examples from this area that appear in museums and private collections. However, the lateness of European contact in this area and the greater scientific interest in its material culture led to the preservation of a greater

proportion of sculptures from this area than from many regions that were subdued earlier.

The Bushongo kingdom, known to other African tribes
as the Bakuba, resulted from a migration from the north of
a strong, politically conscious tribe or group of tribes. They
overcame the loosely organized inner-Congo tribes and im-
posed on them their strongly centralized political structure.
But they borrowed from these conquered tribes their art
forms and other cultural elements. Bushongo legends reveal
that they were more historically minded than most other
African tribes. They had recorded, for example, up to 1905
the names of one hundred and twenty-one kings. In many
instances, moreover, events or happenings relevant to these
kings were associated with this genealogical record.

It is possible as a result of certain of these recorded events
to assign approximate dates to the reigns of Bushongo kings.
An important example is the recording of a total eclipse of
the sun in the reign of the ninety-eighth king. The date of
this event is fixed scientifically as 1680. It is therefore possible to assign the approximate date of 1600 to the reign of
Shamba Bolongongo, whom tradition records as the ninety-
third king. He appears to have been by African standards a
liberal ruler who introduced a number of cultural changes.
In his youth he traveled extensively throughout the Congo
area, and he is credited with having brought the art of weaving to the Bushongo from the west. He was a peace-loving
king who sponsored the development of the arts. Perhaps
his greatest contribution to Bushongo sculpture was the in-
novation of the royal portrait figure. In his lifetime he had a
portrait figure of himself sculptured so that his people could
in later years be encouraged by it in times of adversity. This
seems to have established a precedent that was followed by
later kings. Thirteen royal portrait statues, including that
of Shamba Bolongongo, have been identified more or less
certainly at the present time.

The Shamba Bolongongo figure established the type that
was followed in all succeeding royal-portrait statues. The
pose of these Bushongo figures recall the Lower Congo commemorative ancestor figures. Like them, these kings are represented as seated tailor fashion on a plinth. They wear the

curious flat board-like crown of the Bushongo kings, as well
as the appropriate articles of decoration, such as cowrie shell
belts and armlets, and metal bracelets, shoulder and neck
rings. A short sword, the insignia of office, is held in the
left hand, and in front of the figure a small object is carved
to symbolize an important event that occurred in the reign
of the king or a contribution that was made by him. The
proportions of Bushongo figures are far heavier than are
those of the Lower Congo, the pose is more static, and the
design more compact. The forms, less generalized than
those of the western figures and more naturalistic, are so
ample in scale and so completely knit together organically
that Bushongo carvings give an impression of heaviness.
This effect is a result of the scaling of parts, such as a large
torso, a short neck, and a massive head. The head, from the
chin to the crown, is egg-shape, wide at the forehead and at
the brows. The features of the face are carved in high relief
on the surface of the head. They are large in scale and
widely spaced, and the eyes are half closed, similar to those
of Bayaka and Bapende sculptures, the eyebrows clearly
defined, the nose large and fleshy, and the mouth represented as closed and full-lipped.

Bushongo figures are generic portraits of African divine
kingship, expressing aloofness, severity, and strength. Indi-
vidually they show slight modifications in proportions and
details, to bring the type into relationship with the peculiar-
ities of the king represented. All these figures are carved in
very hard wood, the surface carefully finished and given a
high polish. Few African works are as descriptively individual as these figures, and few express more successfully the
timeless composure, the grandeur of carved shapes and the
monumentality of related masses.

The likelihood that Shamba Bolongongo conceived the
idea and the pose for these figures during his travels in
the west suggests that it came from the Lower Congo tradition. Similarly, the great number of wooden cups from the
Central Congo region makes one wonder whether the
Bushongo might not have acquired this type of carving from
the west, since the style of many of these cups is in the
Bayaka-Bapende tradition. It must be remembered that the

Bushongo were a confederated group of tribes that spread out over a large area of the Central Congo. Many of them certainly had trade relations with their neighbors, and the diffusion of elements must have been considerable and must have worked both ways. The so-called effigy and the geometrically carved cups have obvious Bushongo style features. They are carefully carved in a very hard wood that is highly polished and is decorated by a relief technique with designs that are analogous to those of the raffia-pile textiles of these peoples (Pl. 88). Boxes of various shapes and sizes were similarly decorated in this area (Pl. 86). By the richness of their motives, the boldness of their designs, and the magnificence of their technique, these carved cups and boxes represent the finest examples of African decorative sculpture.

The types of mask used by the Bushongo were, according to tradition, largely borrowed from their neighbors. They are large, polychromed, and very dramatic in design. It is evident, from a comparison with other Central Congo masks, that there was a strong mask tradition in this region. This tradition cut across tribal lines and produced a style of mask typical of the area. A rich and dramatically used polychromy characterizes this style. Despite variations in the size and details of design, Central Congo masks are dynamic in expression and bold in the contrast of their sculptural parts.

It seems likely that Bushongo masks were acquired from many areas within the Central Congo region. A distinctive type of mask was used, for example, by the Bakete, a sub-Bushongo tribe, and by an eastern migrant group of Bapende. Many of these masks are small, often diamond shape, and exhibit striking color juxtapositions of red, white, black, and ochre. They were worn or exhibited during the boys' initiation rites. Many of them are animal or semi-animal in appearance, with short or very long horns that are often carved separately and attached to the head. Facial planes are frequently flat, and the eyes and mouth are carved in high relief, often as tubular forms. The technique of these Central Congo masks is frequently very rough, and it is obvious that considerable emphasis was placed on the

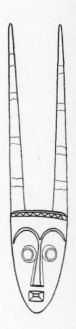

painted surfaces for the desired dramatic effect. A like use of polychromy appears in Bena Lulua sculpture to the northeast. Bena Lulua masks, however, are larger and have a more fully developed dramatic expressiveness.

The most characteristic of Bushongo masks were those used by the Babembe Secret Society. They were made of wood or bark, and the surface was richly painted in small geometric designs suggestive of weaving patterns and often profusely decorated with cowrie shells and beads. A continuous strip of beaded decoration often extends from the bridge of the nose to the point of the chin. A more dramatic type of mask, the "Bombo," was worn during initiation rites, a borrowed trait among the Bushongo. It consisted of a sharply protruding rounded forehead, a narrow face, and a prognathous chin, the entire facial surface elaborately painted with parallel design elements. This mask was said to have been based on Pygmy skulls and was worn to frighten women and the uninitiated away from the enclosure where the initiation rites were taking place. The Pygmies figure prominently in Bushongo mythology and legend as terrifying beings. This has historical basis, for the Pygmies with their poison arrows, were invisible instruments of destruction with which the Bushongo in the early days of their migration into the Central Congo area could not cope. The "Bombo" mask is strikingly like those used by neighboring tribes to the south and southeast and was probably a borrowed Bushongo form.

Although many of the forms and designs of their art are derivative, the Bushongo, with their accomplished technique, refined and enriched the borrowed elements and developed one of the most distinctive Central African styles. A number of substyles in this area show a strong Bushongo influence.

To the east and southeast the sculpture of the Bena Lulua, a Baluba tribe, represents another important Central Congo style. Small standing male and female figures, many only six inches high, are characteristic of this art (Pls. 90–91). Their proportions are slender and elongated and are composed of short heavy legs, long slim bodies, very long necks, and a large distinctively shaped head, usually sur-

mounted by a crested headdress. They are often roughly
shaped, but an elaborate surface decoration is always carefully carved. Facial scarification designs and details of costume are depicted in low relief. Concentric circles are frequently used as stylizations of shoulder, elbow, and knee
joints, and many figures have an elaborately decorated neck,
the carving sometimes suggesting a beaded collar, sometimes a scarification design. The head shape of Bena Lulua
figures is long and broad, with a wide almost bulbous cranium. Of the facial features the most noteworthy are the
huge eyes that are carved with a very large half-closed upper
lid. In many instances, male figures have a short beard that
is elegantly braided in thin strands. Bena Lulua figure style
stresses decorative detail and minimizes weight or mass.

The meaning and function of many of these sculptures is
not known with certainty. Some of them are obviously fetishes (Pls. 91–92); others are probably commemorative ancestor figures. The majority of them were rubbed with red
camwood powder (tukula), which had magical implica-
tions if not power, and it therefore seems that these sculptures may have functioned as fetishes or as charms. Both
fetishism and ancestor worship existed among these people.

Bena Lulua masks are spectacular, colorful, and unrelated to their figure style. They are of the same generic type
as the "Bombo" masks of the Bushongo, who, according to
tradition, acquired some of their masks from the Bena
Lulua. What little is known of the meaning and use of these
masks suggests that they were similarly used as those of the
Bushongo. The influence of Bena Lulua style appears in a
number of substyles in the south-central Congo area, while
there are certain stylistic ties between it and the major styles
to the east and southeast.

East of the Bena Lulua, the Basonge tribes, also of Baluba
origin, created a distinctive art that is best represented by
comparatively small standing fetish figures (Pls. 93–94). In
this style proportions are short and heavy, the forms solidly
and carefully carved, and the legs sharply flexed, giving an
angular rhythm to the figures. The heads are very large,
round or almost squarish in shape, with a wide rounded
cranium similar to those of the Bena Lulua type. Eyes are

large, widely spaced, and sometimes inlaid with shell or metal. The mouth, perhaps the most characteristic feature of this style, is open, but is pinched together in the center, forming a horizontal figure-eight design with a grimacing effect. The very long neck recalls a like feature of the Bena Lulua style and is sometimes carved with a number of widely spaced concentric rings. There are usually no scarification marks on these figures, but pieces of metal or shell are frequently inlaid on the surface. Magical substances are inserted in a cavity in the top of the head, and a small horn or a carved wooden horn is used as a covering of this area. Basonge fetishes are carved by fetishers, some of whom are more skilled than others. These sculptures are therefore uneven in quality. But all of the Basonge figures have an aggressive, menacing expression, to which the angular rhythms and massiveness contribute.

The art tradition of the Central Congo area contains many heterogeneous elements and reaches its highest point in the superb sculptural style of the Bushongo. Polychromed masks are typical of this region, which must be considered one of the few African areas where color is of paramount stylistic importance. Typical, too, of this area is the presence of a considerable number of minor or substyles that show obvious relationships with the more important major styles.

EASTERN CONGO   The sculpture of the East Congo area, between the Lualaba River and Lake Tanganyika, also represents a number of distinct but related styles. The most important is that of the Baluba tribes. Their style is one of the most aesthetically significant of Central Africa. The entire East Congo area is dominated by Baluba culture and traditions. Three types of carvings best illustrate this art: standing figures, stools carved with human supporting figures, and seated or kneeling figures holding a bowl.

Three substyles may be distinguished in this sculpture. They are all based on the same principles, but differ in minor respects. These substyles may be designated on the basis of geographical areas as the Warua, the Manyema, and the East Baluba. The Manyema is a district lying west of the

north-central shore of Lake Tanganyika. The Warua area
is to the south of the Manyema district, and that of the East
Baluba is along the southern shore of Lake Tanganyika.
Each of these substyles, although sharing a number of common elements, evidences clearly distinguishable style features.

Standing female ancestor figures are the finest examples
of Warua art. They are posed in a balanced, completely
frontal manner, the arms flexed, and the hands supporting
the breasts. In proportions they recall somewhat those of
Bena Lulua figures and build up from short sturdy legs,
through an elongated torso, to a large head. But these forms
are carefully carved to express volume and weight. The
slenderness of the torso is shaped to fit down between the
hips; the breasts are small, but full; the navel protrudes;
and the lower part of the abdomen is profusely decorated
with an elaborate scarification design. The shoulders are
wide, rounded, and hunched up; the neck a moderately
short, finely shaped cylinder; and frontally the head is almost completely circular. A band of fine parallel vertical
incisions defines the hairline and marks off a high-domed
forehead from the type of Baluba coiffure characteristic of
this district. This consists of a deep bamboo framework
over which the hair is drawn at the back in a cross pattern.
Facial features are placed low, widely spaced eyes are carved
with heavily hooded lids, the nose is full and flat, and the
mouth is represented by thin protruding lips. A very short
chin appears below the mouth. The design of the head is
composed of a rhythmic pattern of elegant curvilinear
forms. In Warua style figures surface planes flow with great
refinement into one another, allowing full expression to
sensitive oval shapes. Body forms are interpreted as balanced cylindrical shapes. The finest examples of these figures are among the great masterpieces of African Negro
sculpture. Similar sculptures are used decoratively on bow-
rests, axes (Pl. 104), and, with certain adjustments, as supporting figures for neck-rests (Pl. 105) and stools (Pl. 102),
and as free-standing figures holding a bowl (Pl. 101).

Manyema style is well illustrated by carved stools and
figures supporting a bowl. These sculptures have slender,

almost emaciated proportions, and long narrow heads. They express structure rather than volume. In contrast to Warua carvings, they are without flowing surfaces and line patterns. The cheek bones, bridge of the nose, and the bony character of the forehead are stressed by the modeling of the carved surface so that it may catch and utilize the possibilities of light-and-shade effects. Facial features are differently shaped from those of Warua figures. The eyes, for example, are smaller and are short pointed ovals; the nose is narrow, long, and high-bridged, with strongly modeled nostrils. The mouth is a long, full-lipped protuberance. Manyema figures are distinguished by a particular type of hairdress. This consists of a light wooden frame over which the hair is pulled back to form a large petal-like design. Many Manyema figures do not have the smoothness of surface finish or the careful treatment of detail of Warua carvings. A nostalgic sadness of expression replaces the serene calmness of Warua figures. But both styles show a like feeling for organic form.

It seems certain that Manyema and Warua free-standing sculptures represent ancestor figures. Small fetishes and charms were also carved in both styles. Many of them were formerly carved in ivory, of which the finest are the Warua female half-figures that are sculptured out of hippopotamus teeth.

The two most important types of Baluba carvings are represented by the stool figures and by those supporting bowls. They appear in all three styles. The bowl figures, measuring less than two feet high, usually represent a seated or kneeling female figure supporting a bowl. They are carefully carved, and, although used differently, they have a common basic meaning. Some, for example, are carved to honor a respected mendicant or begging spirit (Pl. 101). These are placed at certain times by their owners in front of his house, so that persons passing by may drop shells or other objects of value into the bowl in honor of the spirit. A similar figure was also placed outside the hut during the period of childbirth, when the equivalent of money was again dropped into the bowl by persons passing by. The household was thus compensated for the loss of the services of the woman during this period. The carving therefore commemorated the nobility of motherhood or functioned as a symbol of that respected state. It seems likely that this type of begging or mendicant figure may have been related at one time to ancestor worship, the carving symbolizing the revered mothers among the tribal ancestors.

Mendicant figures also sometimes served another purpose. The bowl held the magical white earth used by sorcerers. In this context, the carved figure probably represented either the spirit contacted by the sorcerer or the origin of his power. It is certain that all mendicant type figures had, however used, a basically religious meaning.

Baluba carved stools and neck-rests (Pls. 102, 105) are, on the contrary, in general decorated objects of utility. They are made for the chief or the important persons of a tribe or village and must be considered as prestige objects. The neck-rests average six inches and the stools two feet in height. A very hard, close-grained wood is often used for these carvings, although in some areas a soft, light, white wood is used. This is stained a dull black. Caryatid-like human figures, male or female, are used in both of these objects in a characteristically functional and decorative manner. The stem of the neck-rest or stool consists of a standing, kneeling, or sometimes seated figure that rests on a circular base and supports on its head the circular seat of the stool or the carved top of the neck-rest (Pls. 102, 105). The arms are frequently held so that the hands of the figure furnish additional support for the top. These caryatid-like figures are often so successfully designed that they do not appear burdened by the weight they support.

Stools, neck-rests, and mendicant figures are also characteristic of the East Baluba style. This is basically derived from that of the Warua. It handles the obvious features of Warua style, however, in such an exaggerated, stiff manner that it is apparent that they were not understood. The technique is also frequently crude. With a few conspicuous exceptions, East Baluba examples are aesthetically and expressively mere travesties of western Baluba sculpture.

Baluba style is further represented by one of the most spectacular of Congo masks, the "Kifwebe." It was also ex-

tensively used by the Basonge and in a modified form by the
Bena Lulua, the two Central Congo tribes of Baluba origin.
The design of this mask varies considerably. In some examples it is a wide oval shape (Pl. 98), in others it is a long,
more nearly diamond, shape (Pls. 96–97, 99). The features
are also variable, and are either carved on the surface or
project from it. But in every case the surface is covered with
a series of curvilinear or rectilinear parallel lines, which are
usually picked out with white earth. These masks are often
large in size and impressive in scale. Many of them are used
by the Lion Secret Society, a political organization that is
an important source of anti-European propaganda activ-
ity.

The true center of the Kifwebe type of mask seems to
have been in the eastern part of the Central Congo area.
But a large type of helmet mask is entirely distinctive of the
Baluba of this region. This mask, usually carved with a
pair of horns suggesting those of the buffalo, is related
stylistically to the sculpture of the Warua style. Smooth
surfaces emphasize volumes and facial features are carved
as carefully as those of Warua style figures. These masks are
carved in a hard wood and are stained a monochromed
black. The exact meaning and purpose of them is not
known, but it is believed that they were used in funerary
rites and may, therefore, have been associated with ancestor
rites.

Another important Eastern Congo style is that of the
non-Baluba Warega tribes. They live in the northeastern
part of this area, and their small wood and ivory carvings,
although distinctive, show a number of Baluba influences.
This is particularly true of their wood carvings. These evidence a more staccato and less skillful rendering of the basic
principles of Baluba style. They replace, for example, the
sensitive and refined expressiveness of the latter style by
broken volumes and line patterns and by a rough surface
effect.

Warega style is, nevertheless, important. It seems apparent that it developed under the combined influences of two
radically different traditions, namely, the Baluba of the
Eastern Congo area and the less technologically advanced
sculptural styles of the Great Lakes region east of the Congo.

The finest examples of Warega style appear in their ivory carvings, such as small masks and neck-rests (Pls. 106–108). Characteristic of a hard resistant material, planes are simplified or angular in definition, and subtle surface detail is absent. It is probable that ivory carving was an old medium among the Warega and that wood sculpture has been a fairly recent development, a new and borrowed technique.

The most distinguished style of the Eastern Congo area is that of the Warua. Its influences were strong and far reaching. Manyema art, although exceptionally strong aesthetically and expressively, was probably a local style that developed within a small area and exerted a limited influence. It seems likely, in fact, that the Manyema style represents the work of one great master sculptor or of a few generations of sculptors who carried on his work. This conclusion seems justified because of the remarkable stylistic similarity between examples of Manyema art.

SOUTHERN CONGO   In the southern part of Central Africa a number of local sculptural styles show an extension of the stronger Congo traditions to the north. For example, the Balunda style in the northeastern part of this area may at best be considered a vitiated and dull echo of Central and East Congo styles. The most important sculpture of this region is that of the Badjokwe tribes. These migrant and warlike people live in a wide area extending from the Kasai-Sankuru district of the Central Congo as far south as the northern part of Angola. Their art evidences a clearly developed style that appears in small free-standing figures, ceremonial staff-heads, masks, and carved stools and chairs.

Badjokwe sculpture is heavily stylized and dramatic and aggressive in expression. A characteristic feature of the style is its animation of pose and expression. Figures, for example, have sharply flexed knees, as though they were moving, and the arms are often bent at the elbows and hold an object, such as a staff or a weapon. Angular rhythms frequently result from the pose of these figures. But body forms are clearly defined and integrated in an organic manner. The shaping of the head is peculiar to Badjokwe style (Pl. 113). It usually consists of a narrow vertical oval face, framed by a wide curving headdress. This headdress pro-

jects in high relief beyond the surface of the face and extends as a roughly rectangular form with considerable depth. In many examples it is developed as a heavy continuous curve at the back of the head. The features of the face are active and aggressive, the mouth often shaped as a large open oval, with teeth represented. Although many of these figures are very small, they all have an impressive scale. The style lacks the finish and the sensitivity of Baluba sculptures, but has instead a strong dramatic expressiveness.

Heads carved on ceremonial staffs are among the finest examples of Badjokwe art (Pl. 113). They are carved in a hard close-grained wood, so highly polished that a metallic effect is achieved. They are also more carefully carved than are the majority of Badjokwe sculptures. This is particularly evident in the definition of form, especially that of the encircling headdress, and in the precise handling of line to describe facial features and separate the various elements of the design.

Few types of mask were carved by this tribe. The most important of them were apparently used in secular dances when men and women alternately mimicked one another. In consequence, those worn by the women have a stylized beard carved at a right angle from the chin and those by the men are small, with small delicately carved features. The finest are distinguished by a careful technique, particularly evident in the elegantly shaped forms and in the lightly carved linear surface designs. Many, however, are very roughly carved; but the best examples are comparable aesthetically to the finest of African masks.

The Badjokwe also decorated with figure sculptures many stools, chairs, neck-rests, and other utilitarian objects (Pls. 109–112). These are usually carved in a hard wood and have a characteristically high polish. The decorative forms are often given a carefully planned rhythmic arrangement, and they, too, have the dynamic pose and dramatic expressiveness so typical of this style.

NORTHERN CONGO Several unique sculptural styles were developed in the northeastern part of the Congo area, in the vicinity of the Uele and Ubangi rivers. The most important

is that of the Mangbetu tribes. Their art includes wood
carvings and modeled ceramic wares. Of the latter, the so-
called effigy jars are accomplished examples (Pls. 114, 115).
They are small jars with the spout, neck, and body of the
jar modeled to represent a human head or torso. Mangbetu
wood carvings comprise a number of figures in the round
that are used decoratively as knife handles, on the lids of
circular boxes (Pl. 116), and as portions of musical instruments. The human head alone is frequently used. Although
details vary slightly from area to area, a constant aspect of
this style is the long narrow head that is based naturalistically on the custom of these people to deform the head by
binding.

Mangbetu ceramics represent the highest development
of this art in Negro Africa. Their pottery vessels range from
about eight inches to more than two feet in height. There
are two types: those of geometric shape and those fash-
ioned as human heads. The majority of the geometric type
objects are elongated vase-like vessels with strongly pro-
nounced reverse curves defining their profiles. The surfaces
are often decorated with etched designs that are composed
of parallel angular or curvilinear elements. Small circular
depressions also appear in these decorations. The geometric
vessels are given a dull black glaze, but the effigy jars are
without this glaze and have a mottled red, gray, and yellow
coloration. Some vessels of both types are composed of two
identical parts joined together. The geometric jars are utilitarian objects, but the effigy types were used to contain the
palm wine which was drunk during the boys' initiation
rites.

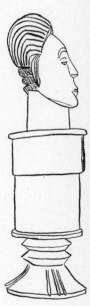

Cylindrical boxes are also typical of Mangbetu art (Pl.
116). They average about two feet in height and were originally made of bark and wood. They are composed of two
parts: the body of the box, and a short covering lid. The
body consists of a cylinder of bark attached to a circular
wooden base that is carved as geometric or human-shape
legs. A narrow cylinder of bark is also attached to a circular
wooden top to form the lid, the wooden top usually carved
as a large human head and neck. These heads are typically
Mangbetu. The long tapering cranium is often carved with

deeply incised lines in simulation of hair. The curvature of the face is, in profile, strongly convex, the forehead very low, and the facial features large in scale. These features, so distinctive of the style, include sharply pointed closed oval eyes, a long flat nose, and a large, protruding mouth, usually with the upper lip overhanging the lower. Large stylized ears are placed at right angles to the sides of the head and are pierced through the center, not through the lobes.

The heads that decorate the boxes do not usually have an elaborately flaring hour-glass shape coiffure as do those on the modeled jars. Heads of both types, however, are carved on the handles of knives and on the stringed musical instruments used by these people. An exceedingly hard, close-grained wood was used in their decorative art. It was usually not painted, but seems to have been lightly oiled so as to produce a light brown color and a slightly polished surface. Some of the musical instruments have the sounding box and the long arms designed as full-length human figures. The handles of the knives are sometimes carved as half figures. This is also true of some of the modeled jars.

Characteristic elements of this style likewise appear in a few free-standing wooden figures, usually female, of about eighteen inches high. The proportions of these figures are more naturalistic than is common in African sculpture. Poses are frontal and fairly static. The forms are heavy and compact, surfaces smooth, and the details are realistic. In some of these figures facial features and incised surface details are at least partially achieved by burning. These details, therefore, stand out as slightly blackened against the light wood. This "poker technique" is also apparent in some of the carvings on the circular boxes and knife-handles.

The Mangbetu wooden figures are said to have been carved solely as aesthetic objects. Peculiar to their art is its lack of religious meaning. It is almost entirely secular and decorative. The greater part of it was made for the upper social classes, and therefore it had sociological significance as evidences of prestige and rank. A number of ivory carvings, some of them echoing the old style, are made today as both prestige and trade items.

Mangbetu style dominates the art of the Northern Congo

area. West and southwest of this region a few local sculptural styles of meager aesthetic quality may be discerned.
Examples of these are the simplified geometric cylindrical
figures of the Bangala tribe, who live between the Ubangi
and the Congo rivers to the west, and the rustic carvings of
the Bapoto, who live east of the Bangala along the Congo
River.

The art of Central Africa shows as great a diversity of
styles as does that of West Africa. But many of these styles
are restricted to smaller tribal groups and do not have as extensive geographical distribution as do those of West Africa.
The small tribal styles of Central Africa are, on the other
hand, often closely interrelated. A considerable degree of
homogeneity is therefore typical of the sculpture of this vast
area.

V EAST AFRICA

To THE EAST AND SOUTH of Central Africa, particularly in Tanganyika, Rhodesia, and Swaziland, there is a large region that may be called for convenience the East African art area. Comparatively little art was produced there, and only a few distinctive styles were developed. Several local traditions may, however, be discerned. The art is best represented by decoratively carved neck-rests, bowls, and shields. Practically no human figures were sculptured, and only a few masks, although simplified animal forms were carved decoratively on bowls and neck-rests in a few regions.

The Makonde, who live in the southeastern portion of what is now Tanganyika, developed one of the few tribal styles of East Africa. They were the only people in this area who carved human figures and masks. There art is therefore somewhat of an oasis of figure sculpture in the midst of simplified abstract design styles.

The few human figures carved in the round by the Makonde are usually full-length standing females. They are sculptured in a light-colored soft wood, some of them unpainted and others stained a light red. The sturdy forms, the stiff poses, and the rather naturalistic proportions suggest comparison with Northern Congo style. The naturalistic details of these figures are also comparable to similar features of the Mangbetu style. Many of them, for example, are carved with a labret or lip-plug, characteristic of these people. Tribal scarification designs are usually represented by incised lines. The marked variations in the style of these figures, particularly apparent in the rendering of facial features, indicates that they did not develop from a single strong tradition. There is, therefore, a lack of style unity in these Makonde sculptures. Their meaning and purpose is not clearly known.

Makonde masks, on the other hand, share a number of
distinctive style elements. There are several types of masks,
some apparently male, and others female, the latter identified by the presence of the lip-plug. Both types are often
described by wide oval shapes, the ears projecting at each
side as flat segments of an oval. Facial planes are flat or
slightly depressed, the nose narrow and long, the eyes often
small square holes, and the lips slightly projecting and divided by a narrow slit. Some of the masks are painted, as are
the figures, a dark monochrome red and have human hair
inserted in the top of the head. Usually no carved decoration is found on Makonde masks, but some of them are decorated with small round patches of red, white, and blue
beads that are attached to the wooden surface by means of a
wax or resinous base.

Makonde masks were worn during the boys' puberty rites.
It is said that some of the wearers danced on stilts. They
represent a distinctive style of African mask. They express
alertness, but they lack the dramatic aggressiveness and the
impressive spectacular quality of many Central Congo
masks. They have a sculpturally simple style, but it is rich
in rhythmic line patterns and boldly contrasting surfaces.

An equally characteristic East African style appears in
the decorated bowls of the Barotse, who live along the Zambesi River in the present political area of Northern Rhodesia. These are utilitarian objects of prestige value. The
style is distinguished by simplicity and clarity of form and
line. The bowls are carved in a soft light wood and are
stained a flat dull black. Some of them are small, but many
are more than two feet long. The preferred and usual shape
is an ovoid with the top and bottom flattened. They are
made in two parts, the body of the bowl proper and a shallow lid, the body being deep, with thick sides and a heavy
lip into which the lid fits. The body of the bowl is usually
plain, but the geometric shapes evidence in
their sureness of form an accomplished technique and a feeling for abstract sculptural
volumes. The only decoration often appears
on the lid. Here a group of animals are usually
carved in the round, including water buffaloes,

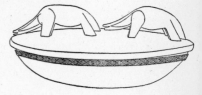

elephants, and wild ducks. Three or more forms are evenly
and rhythmically arranged in a single row, frequently with
the central figure larger and the forms at the front and
the back progressively smaller. The carvings are extremely
simplified renderings of animal forms and owe their aesthetic interest largely to their rhythmical interrelationships.
These decorative sculptures are basically functional and
serve as a handle for the lid.

A similar feeling for geometric form and rhythmic line
also appears in the Barotse neck-rests (Pl. 117). They are
usually carved from a hard wood, and many of them have a
smooth streamlined elegance of design. Many of these neck-
rests have a small water-buffalo or other naturalistic form
carved as a stem between the bottom and the top. The animal form is comparable in its simplicity of handling to those
on the carved bowls. Other Barotse neck-rests are geometric
in design, but the sequence and harmony of lines and shapes
give these carvings an aesthetic quality.

In some regions of East Africa neck-rests are carved with a
stylized antelope form as a central support. Among the
Zulu and Swazi tribes to the south, however, a geometric
type of neck-rest is common (Pl. 118). These are distinguished by a strongly marked feeling for rhythmic designs
and harmonious elements. This is also evident, in fact, in
the carved and painted wooden shields of this area. They
often have concentric circular or angular patterns symmet-
rically arranged in a rhythmic design.

The art of East Africa is composed largely of simplified
naturalistic and geometric elements. Its aesthetic effects result from a rhythmic and symmetrical arrangement of forms
and lines. In style it is unrelated to that of other parts of
Negro Africa. East African art is almost exclusively a decorative art and lacks the religious and political significance
common to African sculpture in other areas. But it is, nevertheless, an art of considerable aesthetic quality and one that
is essentially Negro in its sculptural elements.

AFRICAN NEGRO SCULPTURE
IN AMERICAN COLLECTIONS

THE FACT THAT America was not involved in the partition-
ing of Africa in the late nineteenth century meant that examples of African Negro art did not appear in the normal
course of events in our natural history or ethnological museums. A number of objects, however, were acquired by
traders, explorers, and missionaries. In most cases they form
the basis of American collections. But many of our important collections have been acquired through purchase and
trade during the past thirty or forty years. A surprisingly
large number of excellent examples have been acquired in
this way. The majority are in natural history or scientific
museums, where they are often, unfortunately, poorly exhibited; in some instances, largely because of lack of space,
they are not exhibited at all. In only a few cases are African
sculptures displayed as examples of native art. There is,
however, an increasing awareness of the aesthetic quality of
these objects by those to whom they are entrusted. It is not
surprising, therefore, that these sculptures are readily lent
to "art exhibitions." Many institutions, in fact, are looking
forward to the day when they can exhibit these carvings as
art objects. Persons interested in the collections not on dis-
play, but in the storerooms of the various museums, may
upon application to the proper authorities have access to
the storerooms where these surplus objects are housed.

African sculpture in American collections may be listed
as follows.

MUSEUMS WITH VERY EXTENSIVE COLLECTIONS

Philadelphia, Penna., Museum of the University of
Pennsylvania: a general collection of excellent quality.

This is one of the most important American collections, although there are a few areas not represented there.

Cambridge, Mass., Peabody Museum, Harvard University: a large general collection, with many objects of exceptional merit, especially those of the Poro and Fang styles. There are also a number of good examples of East African styles.

Toronto, Ontario, Canada, Royal Ontario Museum of Archaeology: a very extensive good general collection, with many unique objects from West Africa. The greater number of fine sculptures, however, are from the Central, Eastern, and Southern Congo areas. It is one of the important and representative American collections.

New York, N.Y., American Museum of Natural History: particularly strong in fine Congo material, although a number of areas of West Africa are not represented.

Buffalo, N.Y., Buffalo Museum of Science: many excellent objects from the majority of important areas.

Chicago, Ill., Chicago Natural History Museum: an extensive collection, with a good deal of ethnological material from Angola and Nigeria. Of exceptional interest are the very fine Cameroon sculptures.

INSTITUTIONS WITH MEDIUM-SIZE COLLECTIONS

Denver, Colorado, The Denver Art Museum: a moderately small collection, with some excellent examples. This is growing and will probably become one of the important African collections.

Evanston, Ill., Department of Anthropology, Northwestern University, the Bascom and Herskovits collections: many very important examples of Dahomey, Yoruba, and Niger Delta art.

Brooklyn, N.Y., Brooklyn Museum: an excellently exhibited collection, small, but with some very fine examples.

New York, N.Y., New York Public Library, The Schomburg Collection (104 West 136th Street): a comparatively small number of Congo sculptures, many of them of very high quality.

Philadelphia, Penna., Commercial Museum: contains a few old and important pieces.

Newark, N.J., Newark Museum: a small number of objects of outstanding interest.

Washington, D.C., United States National Museum, Smithsonian Institution: an assorted collection, poorly displayed, but with some pieces of genuinely fine quality.

Salem, Mass., Peabody Museum of Salem: a very small collection, with a few old and remarkably fine objects.

SOURCES FOR REPRODUCTIONS

Sizable photographs of good quality and a number of postcard sets may be had of many objects in American museums. When the object has already been photographed, these prints can be secured at moderate cost. The Museum of the University of Pennsylvania has a small illustrated publication on its collection, and the Chicago Natural History Museum has published in their Guide Series an illustrated book of the Ethnology of Africa. Of particular interest are a number of moderately priced plaster casts of excellent quality which may be secured from the Museum of the University of Pennsylvania. A small illustrated catalogue of these casts is published and may be obtained from them.

SELECTED BIBLIOGRAPHY

THE FOLLOWING BIBLIOGRAPHY includes references to background material, discussions of specific areas or objects, and sources for illustrations. It is arranged to follow the divisions and art areas set forth in the text.

GENERAL

Adam, L. Primitive Art. London, 1949.

Anti, Carlo. Sculpture of the African Negroes, *Art in America,* XII (1923), 14–26.

Apollinaire, G., and P. Guillaume. Sculptures nègres. Paris, 1917.

Baesler, A. L'Art chez les peuples primitifs. Paris, 1929.

Barr, A. H. Antiquity of African Sculpture, *Museum of Modern Art Bulletin,* II (1935), 3.

Bell, Clive. Negro Sculpture, *Living Age,* CCCVI (1920), 786–789.

—— Negro Sculpture, *Arts and Decoration,* XIII (1920), 178–202.

—— Since Cézanne: Negro Sculpture. London, 1922.

Bernatzik, H. A., ed., Afrika; Handbuch der Angewandten Völkerkunde. 2 vols. Innsbruck, 1942.

British Museum. Handbook to the Ethnographical Collections. 2d ed. London, 1925.

Carline, R. The Dating and Provenance of Negro Art, *Burlington Magazine,* LXXVII (1940), 115–123.

Chauvet, S. Les Arts indigènes des colonies françaises. Paris, 1924.

—— Objets d'or, de bronze et d'ivoire dans l'art nègre, *Cahiers d'Art,* V (1930), 33–40.

Clawson, H. P. By Their Works. Buffalo, 1941.

Clouzot, H., and A. Level. L'Art nègre, *Gazette des Beaux-Arts,* XV (1919), 311–324.

—— L'Art nègre et l'art océanien. Paris, 1919.

—— Sculptures africaines et océaniennes, Paris, 1926.

Culin, S. Negro Art, *The Arts.* III (1923), 347–350.

—— Negro Art, *Brooklyn Museum Quarterly,* X (1923), 119–132.

Cunard, Nancy, ed. Negro: an Anthology. London, 1934.

Delafosse, M. The Negroes of Africa (tr. by F. Flegelman). Washington, 1931.

Einstein, Carl. Negerplastik. Munich. 1920.

—— Afrikanische Plastik. Berlin, n.d.

—— La Sculpture africaine. Paris, 1922.

—— A propos de l'Exposition de la Galeria Pigalle, *Documents,* No. 2, 1930, pp. 104–112.

Fels, F. Les Arts sauvages à la Galerie Pigalle, *L'Art Vivant,* VI (1930), 228–232.

Frobenius, L. Die Masken und Geheimbunde Afrikas. Halle, 1898.

—— The Voice of Africa. 2 vols. London, 1913.

—— Das unbekannte Afrika. Munich, 1923.

—— L'Art africain, *Cahiers d'Art,* V (1930), 395–429.

—— Kulturgeschichte Afrikas. Zurich, 1933.

Fry, Roger. Last Lectures. London, 1939.

Fuhrmann, E. Afrika (Kulturen der Erde, 6). Hagen, 1922.

Gallotti, J. Les Arts indigènes a l'Exposition Coloniale, *Art et Décoration,* 1931, pp. 69–100.

Germann, P. Afrikanische Kunst, in A. Springer, *Handbuch der Kunstgeschichte,* 4, Berlin, 1929, pp. 549–588.

Gill, J. W. Handbook and Guide to the African Collection in the Public Museums. Liverpool, 1931.

Gregar, J. Masks of the World. London, 1936–1937.

Griaule, M. Arts de l'Afrique Noire. Paris, 1947.

Guillaume, P., and T. Munro. Primitive Negro Sculpture. N.Y., 1926.

Hall, H. U. Some Examples of African Art, *Journal of the University of Pennsylvania Museum,* X (1919), 77–101.

Hambly, W. D. Ethnology of Africa. Chicago, 1930. Chicago Natural History Museum, Guide, Part 3.

—— Source Book for African Anthropology. 2 vols. Chicago (Chicago Natural History Museum), 1937.

Hardy, G. L'Art nègre. Paris, 1927.

Hausenstein, W. Barbaren und Klassiker. Munich, 1922.

Herskovits, M. J. A Preliminary Consideration of the Culture Areas of Africa, *American Anthropologist,* XXVI (1924), 50–63.

—— The Backgrounds of African Art. Denver (Denver Art Museum), 1945.

Kjersmeier, C. Centres de style de la sculpture Nègre Africaine. 4 vols. Paris, 1935–38.

—— African Negro Sculpture. New York, 1948.

Kuehn, H. Die Kunst der Primitiven. Munich, 1923.

Lederer, P. Primitive Art of Africa . . . in the Collection of Curtis Moffat, *Connoisseur,* XCV (1935), 205–210.

Locke, A. L. African Art: Classic Style, *American Magazine of Art,* XXVIII (1935), 270–278.

Maes, J. Des sources de l'art nègre, *Cahiers d'Art,* V (1930), 307–313.

—— L'Art nègre a l'Exposition du Palais des Beaux-Arts. Brussels, 1930.

Maes, J., and H. Lavachery. L'Art nègre. Brussels, 1930.

Museck, J. B. African Sculptures, *Bulletin of the St. Louis Museum,* XXVII (1942), 45–49.

Olbrechts, F. M. Contribution to the Study of the Chronology of African Plastic Art, *Africa,* XIV (1943), 183–193.

Perkam, M., and J. Simmons. African Discovery. London, 1943.

Portier, A., and F. Ponceton. Les Arts sauvages: Afrique. Paris, 1930.

Ratton, C. Masques africains. Paris, 1931.

Salles, G. Réflexions sur l'art nègre, *Cahiers d'Art,* II (1927), 247–258.

Salmon, A. Negro Art, *Burlington Magazine,* XXXVI (1920), 164–172.

—— L'Art nègre, *Propos d'Atelier.* 1922, pp. 115–136.

Schebesta, P., and G. Höltker. Der afrikanischer Schild, *Anthropos,* XVIII–XIX (1923–1924), 1012–1062; XX (1925), 817–859.

Schweinfurth, G. Artes africainae. Leipzig, 1875.

Seligman, C. G. Races of Africa. London, 1930.

Sevier, M. Negro Art, *Atelier,* II (1931), 116–121.

Springer, A., ed. Die aussereuropaische Kunst. Leipzig, 1929. Handbuch der Kunstgeschichte, 6.

Sweeney, J. J. African Negro Art, Museum of Modern Art. New York, 1935.

Sydow, E. von. Das Tier in der afrikanischen Plastik, *Der Ararat,* II (1921), 206–219.

—— Afrikanische Hilzbildwerke im Leipziger Museum, *Kunstchronik und Kunstmarkt,* LIX (1921), 625–639.

—— Die Kunst der Naturvolker und der Vorzeit. Berlin, 1923.

—— African Sculpture, *Africa,* I (1928), 210–227.

—— Sammlung Baron Eduard von der Heydt. Berlin, 1932.

Szecsi, L. Primitive Negro Art, *Art and Archaeology,* XXXIV (1933), 130–136.

Vatter, E. Religioese Plastik der Naturvoelker. Frankfurt, 1926.

Wieschoff, H. A. The African Collections of the University Museum, *Bulletin of the University of Pennsylvania,* XI (1945), 1–76.

—— An Anthropological Bibliography of Negro Africa. New Haven, 1948.

Wingert, Paul S. African Negro Sculpture. San Francisco, 1948.

Zayas, M. de. Negro Art, *The Arts,* III (1923), 199–205.

Zervos, C. L'Art nègre, *Cahiers d'Art,* II (1927), 229–246.

WEST AFRICA

GENERAL

Balfour, H. Modern Brass Casting in West Africa, *Journal of the Royal Anthropological Institute,* XXXVI (1906), 525–528.

Bernatzik, H. A. Meine Expedition nach Portugiesisch-Guinea, *Atlantis,* IV (1932), 197–211.

Clarke, D. Negro Art: Sculpture from West Africa, *Journal of the Royal African Society,* XXXIV (1935), 129–137.

Olbrechts, Frans M. Notre mission ethnographique en Afrique Occidentale Française, *Bulletin, Musées Royal (Belge) d'Art et d'Histoire,* 3d series, No. 5, 1933, pp. 98–107.

Rivet, P., and G. Rivière. Mission Dakar-Djibouti, 1931–33, *Minotaure,* II (1933), 3–61.

Sadler, M. E. Arts of West Africa. Oxford, 1935.

Sydow, E. von. Westafrikanische Gebrauchkunst, *Cicerone,* XIII (1921), 614–620.

Underwood, L. Figures in Wood of West Africa. London, 1947.

—— Masks of West Africa. London, 1948.

—— Bronzes of West Africa. London, 1949.

SUDAN

Delafosse, M. Haut Senegal Niger. 3 vols. Paris, 1912.

—— Les Nègres. Paris, 1927.

Desplagnes, L. Le Plateau Central Nigerien. Paris, 1907.

Fagg, William. Two Woodcarvings from the Baga of French Guinea, *Man,* XLVII (1947), 105–106.

Griaule, M. Masques dogons, *Travaux et Mémoirs de l'Institut d'Ethnologie de l'Universite de Paris,* Vol. XXXIII (1938).

Hall, H. U. Two Wooden Statuettes from French West Africa, *Journal of the University of Pennsylvania Museum,* XVIII (1927), 175–187.

—— Twins in Upper Guinea, *Journal of the University of Pennsylvania Museum,* XIX (1928), 403–427.

Kjersmeier, C. Habbe-Kunst, *Ymer,* 54 (1934), 59–68.

Lem, F.-H. Sculptures soudanaises. Paris, 1948.

WEST GUINEA COAST

Addison, W. The Nomori of Sierra Leone, *Antiquity,* VIII (1934), 335–338.

Donner, E. Kunst und Handwerk in Ostliberia, Baessler-archiv, 1941.

Eberl-Alber, R. Die Masken der Männerbunde in Sierra Leone, *Ethnos*, II (1937), 38–46.

Glück, J. Die Goldgewichte von Oberguinea. Heidelberg, 1907.

Harley, G. W. Notes on the Poro in Liberia, *Papers of the Peabody Museum of American Archaeology and Ethnology*, Vol. XIX, No. 2 (1941).

Joyce, T. A. Steatite Figures from West Africa in the British Museum, *Man*, V (1905), 97–100.

Migeod, F. W. H. The Poro Society, *Man*, XVI (1916), 102–108.

Neel, H. Statuettes en pierre et en argile de l'Afrique Occidentale, *L'Anthropologie*, XXIV (1913), 419–443.

Parker, H. Stone Circles in Gambia, *Journal of the Royal Anthropological Institute*, LIII (1923), 173–228.

Schwab, G. Tribes of the Liberian Hinterland, *Papers of the Peabody Museum of American Archaeology and Ethnology*, XXXI (1947).

CENTRAL GUINEA COAST

Dellenbach, M. Documents pour l'ethnographie de la côte d'Ivroie: poids pour peser la poudre d'or, *Archives suisses d'Anthropologie général*, VII, No. 1 (1934), 58–72.

Duchartre, Pierre-Louis. Poids et figurines nègres, *Art et Décoration*, LVII (1930), 145–152.

Foote, H. S. Gold Ornament from Ashanti, *Bulletin of the Cleveland Museum of Art*, XXXI (1944), 180–181.

Hall, H. U. Two New West African Sculptures, *Bulletin, University of Pennsylvania Museum*, II (1930), 60–63.

—— West African Masks, *Connoisseur*, XCIII (1934), 380–383.

Himmelheber, H. Negerkünstler. Stuttgart, 1935.

Kjersmeier, C. Ashanti Goldweights. Copenhagen, 1948.

Lavachery, H. Apparent évolution des masques dans la region de Man, *Bulletin of the Musées Royaux (Belge) d'Art et d'Histoire*, 3d series, No. 6, 1939, pp. 137–141.

Meyerowitz, Eva L. R. Some Gold, Bronze and Brass Objects from Ashanti, *Burlington Magazine*, LXXXVI (1947), pp. 18–21.

Neveux, M. Religion des noirs, fetiches de la Côte d'Ivoire, *L'Ethnographie*, VII (1923), 136–165.

Olbrechts, Frans M. Maskers en dansers in de ivoorkunst. Mechelen, 1940.

Rattray, R. S. Ashanti. Oxford, 1923.

—— Religion and Art in Ashanti. Oxford, 1927.

—— The Tribes of the Ashanti Hinterland. 2 vols. Oxford, 1932.

Schweeger-Hefel, A. Afrikanische Bronzen. Vienna, 1948.

Shaw, C. T. Archaeology in the Gold Coast, *African Studies*, II (1943), 139–147.

Tauxier, L. Nègres Gouro et Gagou. Paris, 1924.
—— Etudes soudanaises; religion, mœurs et coutumes des Agnis de la Côte d'Ivoire. Paris, 1932.
Thomas, N. W. Ashanti and Baoule Gold Weights, *Journal of the Royal Anthropological Institute*, L (1920), 52–68.
Wild, R. P. Stone Age Pottery from the Gold Coast and Ashanti, *Journal of the Royal Anthropological Institute*, LXIV (1934), 203–215.
Wild, R. P., and H. J. Braunholtz. Baked Clay Heads from Graves near Fomena, Ashanti, *Man*, XXXIV (1934), 1–4.
Zeller, R. Die Goldgewichte von Asante; eine ethnologische Studie. Baessler-archiv, III (1912), 1–77.

DAHOMEY

Frazer, J. Statues of Three Kings of Dahomey, *Man*, VIII (1908), 130–132.
Griaule, M., and G. Dieterlen. Calebasses dahomeennes, *Journal de la Société des Africanistes*, V (1935), 203–246.
Herisse, A. le. L'Ancienne Royaume de Dahomey. Paris, 1911.
Herskovits, M. J. Some Aspects of Dahomean Ethnology, *Africa*, V (1932), 266–296.
—— Dahomey. 2 vols. New York, 1938.
—— Symbolism in Dahomean Art, *Man*, XLI (1941), 117.
Herskovits, M. J., and F. S. Herskovits. The Art of Dahomey, *American Magazine of Art*, XXVII (1934), 67–76; 124–131.
Merwart, E. O. L'Art dahomeen; collection du Gouverneur Merwart. Marseille, 1922.
Meyerowitz, E., and R. Meyerowitz. Museum in the Royal Palaces of Abomey, Dahomey, *Burlington Magazine*, LXXXIV (1944), 146–149.
Réal, D. Note sur l'art dahomeen, *L'Anthropologie*, XXX (1920), 367–392.

EAST GUINEA COAST

Akpata, A. Notes on Altars and Bronze Heads at Benin, *Ethnologia Cranmorensis*, I (1937), 5–10.
Bascom, W. R. Brass Portrait Heads from Ile-Ife, Nigeria, *Man*, XXXVIII (1938), 176.
Baumann, H., H. Labouret, C. Ratton. Bronzes et ivories du Benin au Musée d'Ethnographie, Palais du Trocadero, *Cahiers d'Art*, Vol. VII (1932).
Baumann, H. Benin, *Cahiers d'Art*, VII (1932), 197–203.
Boulton, L. C. Bronze Artists of West Africa, *American Museum Journal*, XXXVI (1935), 17–22.
Daniel, F. The Stone Figures of Esie, Ilorin Province, Nigeria, *Journal of the Royal Anthropological Institute*, LXVII (1937) 43–49.

Duckworth, E. H., ed. Nigerian Arts and Crafts, *Nigeria,* XIV (1938), 90–172.

Exposition de bronzes et ivories du Royaume de Benin. Paris (Musée d'Ethnographie), 1932.

Fagg, W. The Antiquities of Ife, *Magazine of Art,* XLIII (1950), 129–133.

Field, J. O. Bronze Castings Found at Igbo, Southern Nigeria, *Man,* XL (1940), 1–6.

Galway, H. Benin: Altars and Compounds, *Ethnologia Cranmorensis,* III (1938), 3–5.

Hagen, K. Altertümer von Benin im Museum für Völkerkunde zu Hamburg, 1900–1918, 2 vols.

Hall, H. U. Great Benin Royal Altar, *Journal of the University of Pennsylvania Museum,* XIII (1922), 105–167.

—— An Ivory Standing Cup from Benin, *Journal of the University of Pennsylvania Museum,* XVII (1926), 414–432.

—— A Large Drum from Benin, *Journal of the University of Pennsylvania Museum,* XIX (1928), 130–143.

Hooton, E. A. Benin Antiquities in the Peabody Museum, *Harvard African Studies,* I (1917), 130–146.

Jensen, A. De la technique á employer pour recueillir les poésies africaines [Ife heads], *Cahiers d'Art,* V (1930), 431–443.

Joyce, T. A. Note on the Relation of the Bronze Heads to the Carved Tusks, *Man,* VIII (1908), 2–4.

Labouret, H. Les Bronzes de cire-perdue du Benin, *Cahiers d'Art,* VII (1932), 204–208.

Ling Roth, H. Great Benin. Halifax (England), 1903.

Luschan, F. von. Die Altertümer von Benin. 3 vols. Berlin, 1919.

Macfie, J. W. S. A Shongo Staff, *Man,* XVIII (1913), 169–171.

Marquart, J. Die Benin-Sammlung des Reichsmuseums für Völkerkunde im Leyden, Veroff. des Reichsmuseums für Völkerkunde in Leyden, Ser. 2, No. 7, Leyden, 1913.

Meyerowitz, Eva L. R. Four pre-Portuguese Bronze Castings from Benin, *Man,* XL (1940), 129–132.

—— Ancient Nigerian Bronzes, *Burlington Magazine,* LVII (1941), 89–93.

—— The Stone Figures of Esie in Nigeria, *Burlington Magazine,* LXXXII (1943), 31–36.

—— Ancient Bronzes in the Royal Palace at Benin, *Burlington Magazine,* LXXXIII (1943), 248–253.

—— Wood-carving in the Yoruba Country Today, *Africa,* XIV (1943), 66–70.

—— Notes on the King-God Shango and His Temple at Ibadan, Southern Nigeria, *Man,* XLVI (1946), 25–31.

Meyerowitz, H., and V. Meyerowitz. Bronzes and Terra-cottas

from Ile-Ife, *Burlington Magazine,* LXXV (1939), 150–155.

Olbrechts, Frans M. Notre ivorie sculpture du Benin, *Bulletin des Musées Royaux (Belge) d'Art et d'Histoiré* 3, No. 2, 1931, pp. 51–55.

Palmer, H. R. Gabi Figures from Jebba Island, *Man,* XXXI (1931), 261–262.

—— Ancient Nigerian Bronzes, *Burlington Magazine,* LXXXI (1942), 252–254.

Pitt-Rivers, G. H. Antique Works of Art from Benin. London, 1900.

Ratton, C. Les Bronzes du Benin, *Cahiers d'Art,* VII (1932), 209–216.

Read, C. H. Note on Certain Ivory Carvings from Benin, *Man,* X (1910), 49–51.

Read, C. H., and O. M. Dalton. Antiquities from the City of Benin and Other Parts of West Africa in the British Museum. London, 1897.

—— Works of Art from Benin City, *Journal of the Royal Anthropological Institute,* XXVII (1898), 362–383.

Roth, H. Ling. Great Benin—Its Customs, Art and Horrors. London, 1913.

Struck, B. Die Chronologie der Benin-Altertümer, *Zeitschrift für Ethnologie,* LV (1923), 113–166.

Sydow, E. von. Ancient and Modern Art in Benin City, *Africa,* XI (1938), 55–62.

—— Kunst und Kulte von Benin, *Atlantis,* X (1938), 46–56.

Tremearne, A. J. N. Notes on Nigerian Tribal Marks, *Journal of the Royal Anthropological Institute,* XLI (1911), 162–178.

Walker, S. W. Gabi Figures from Jebba and Tada, Middle Niger, *Man,* XXXIV (1934), 169–172.

NIGER RIVER DELTA

Basden, G. T. Niger Ibos. London, 1938.

Chaldwick, E. R. Wall Decorations of Ibo Houses, *Nigerian Field,* VI (1937), 134–135.

Einstein, C. Masque de danse rituelle Ekoi, *Documents,* VII (1927), 396.

Jeffreys, M. D. W. Some Notes on the Ekoi, *Journal of the Royal Anthropological Institute,* LXIX (1939), 95–108.

—— The Bull-Roarer among the Ibo, *African Studies,* VIII (1949), 23–34.

Jones, G. J. Mbari Houses, *Nigerian Field,* VI (1937), 77–79.

—— Chaffia Obu Houses, *Nigerian Field,* VI (1937), 169–171.

—— On the Identity of Two Masks from Southeastern Nigeria in the British Museum, *Man,* XXXIX (1939), 33–34.

MacGregor, J. K. Some Notes on "Nsibidi" (Ibo "Writing"),

Journal of the Royal Anthropological Institute, XXXIX
(1939), 209–219.

Murray, K. C. Ekpu: the Ancestor Figure of Oran, Southern
Nigeria, *Burlington Magazine,* LXXXIX (1947), 310–314.

—— Ibo Headdresses Combining Human and Animal Features, *Man,* XLVIII (1948), 1–2.

Sydow, E. von. Masques-Janus du Cross-River, *Documents,* No. 6, 1930, pp. 321–328.

—— The Image of Janus in African Sculpture, *Africa,* V (1932), 14–27.

Talbot, P. A. Note on Ibo Houses, *Man,* XVI (1916), 129.

—— The Peoples of Southern Nigeria. 3 vols. Oxford, 1926.

—— Tribes of the Niger Delta. London, 1932.

Thomas, N. W. Some Ibo Burial Customs, *Journal of the Royal Anthropological Institute,* XLVII (1917), 160–212.

Whitehouse, A. A. Note on the "Mbari" Festival, *Man,* IV (1904), 162–163.

CAMEROON

Albert, A. Bandjoon. Ottawa, 1943.

Dalton, O. M. On Carved Doorposts from the West Coast of Africa, *Man,* I (1901), 69.

Germann, P. Das plastisch-figürliche Kunstgewerbe im Graslande von Kamerun, *Jahr. des Museum für Völkerkunde* (Leipzig), IV (1910), 1–35.

Hagen, G. von. Die Bana, *Baessler-archiv,* II (1911), 77–116.

Jeffreys, M. D. W. Notes on Twins: Bamenda, *African Studies,* VI (1947), 189–195.

Labouret, M. H. Catalogue de l'Exposition de la Mission au Cameroun, Musée du Trocadero. Paris, 1935.

Lebeuf, J. P. La Plaine du Tchad et ses arts. Paris, 1946.

Malcolm, L. W. G. Note on Brass-casting in the Central Cameroon, *Man,* XXIII (1923), 1–4.

—— The Tribes of the Grassland Area, Central Cameroon, *Mitteilungen der Anthropologischen Gesellschaft in Wien,* LV (1925), 7–45.

—— Huts and Villages in the Cameroons, *Scottish Geographical Magazine,* XXXVIII (1923), 21–27.

Oldenburg, R. Bamum; ein Negerrsich in Innern Kameruns, *Atlantis,* III (1930), 161–164.

Staschewski, F. Banjangi, *Baessler-archiv,* VIII (1917), 1–66.

Thomas, T. Variation on a Theme: Analysis of Small Carved Figures from Bali, Cameroons, Africa, *Man,* XXXVIII (1938), 33–37.

CENTRAL AFRICA

GENERAL

Anti, C. Scultura negra, *Dedalo,* I (1921), 592–621.

Bastian, A. Die Deutsche Expedition an der Loangoküste. 2 vols. Jena, 1875.

Clouzot, H., and A. Level. L'Art du Congo Belge. Paris, 1921.

—— L'Art du Congo Belge, *Art et Décoration,* XL (1921), 149–160.

Haardt, G. M., and L. Audouin-Dubreuil. Expedition Citroën Centre Afrique, *La Geographie,* XLV (1926), 121–157; 295–331.

Kochnitzky, L. Negro Art in Belgian Congo. New York, 1948.

Locke, A. A Collection of Congo Art, *The Arts,* IX (1927), 61–70.

Maes, J. Figurines commemoratives et allegoriques du Congo Belge, *Ipek* (1928), 77–91.

—— Des Sources de l'art nègre, *Cahiers d'Art,* VI (1930), 307–313.

—— Le Tissage chez les populations du Lac Leopold II, *Anthropos,* XXV (1930), 393–408.

—— La Psychologie de l'art nègre, *Ipek* (1926), 275–283.

Olbrechts, Frans M. Plastiek van Kongo. Antwerp, 1946.

Perier-Gaston, D. L'Art indigène au Congo Belge, *Beaux-Arts,* VIII (1930), 33–36.

Pleasants, F. R. African Sculpture in the Peabody Museum of Cambridge, Mass., *Ipek,* 1936–37, 117–124.

Torday, E. Le Fetichisme, l'idolatrie et le sorcellerie des Bantous Occidentaux, *L'Anthropologie,* XXXIX (1929), 431–454.

Wingert, Paul S. Congo Art, *Transactions, New York Academy of Sciences,* Series 2, IX (1947), 320–337.

NORTHWEST

Allégret, E. Les Idées religieuses des Fan, *Revue de l'Histoire des Religions,* L (1904), 214–233.

Bennett, A. L. Ethnological Notes on the Fang, *Journal of the Royal Anthropological Institute,* II (1899), 66–98.

Chauvet, S. L'Art funeraire au Gabon. Paris, 1933.

Clouzot, H., and A. Level, Afrique Occidentale Française, *La Renaissance,* V (1922), 216–227.

Grébert, M. F. L'Art musical chez les Fang du Gabon, *Archives suisses d'Anthropologie général,* V, No. 1 (1928), 75–86.

—— Arts en voie du disparition au Gabon, *Africa,* VII (1934), 82–88.

Hée, R. P. A. Le Ngo, société secret du Haut-Ogowe (Gabon), *Africa,* X (1937), 472–480.

Martrow, L. Les "Eki" du Fang, *Anthropos*, I (1906), 745–761.

Mullen, B. H. Fetishes from Loudana, Southwest Africa, *Man*, V (1905), 102–104.

Nassau, P. H. Fetishism in West Africa. London, 1904.

Pechuel-Loesche, E. Volkskunde von Loango. Stuttgart, 1907.

Sydow, E. von. Ahnenfiguren aus Französisch-Äquatorial-Afrika, *Der Cicerone*, XX (1930), 214–218.

Tessmann, G. Die Pangwe. 2 vols. Berlin, 1913.

Trezenem, E. Notes ethnographiques sur les tribes Fan du Moyen Ogooué (Gabon), *Journal de la Société des Africanistes*, VI (1936), 65–93.

LOWER CONGO

Bittremieux, L. Mayombsche Volkskunst. Louvain, 1924.

—— La Société secrète Bakhimba au Mayombe. Brussels, 1936.

Hall, H. U. Fetish Figures of Equatorial Africa, *Journal of the University of Pennsylvania Museum*, XI (1920), 27–55.

—— Congo and West African Wood-Carvings, *Journal of the University of Pennsylvania Museum*, XIV (1923), 47–84; 101–134.

—— Congo Fetish and Divining Images, *Journal of the University of Pennsylvania Museum*, XV (1924), 58–69.

—— Two Wooden Statuettes from the Lower Congo, *Journal of the University of Pennsylvania Museum*, XVIII (1927), 99–110.

—— Two Masks from French Equatorial Africa, *Journal of the University of Pennsylvania Museum*, XVIII (1927), 381–409.

Jadot, J. M. L'Art nègre au Congo Belge (1886–1946), *Revue Congo Belge*, XIX (1946), 41–45.

Maes, J. Les Figurines sculptées du Bas-Congo, *Africa*, III (1930), 347–359.

—— Fetischen of Tooverbeelden uit Kongo, *Annales du Musée du Congo Belge* (Tervuren), Series, VI (1935), Vol. I.

Nuoffer, Afrikanische Plastik in der Gestaltung von Mutter und Kind. Dresden, 1925.

Overbergh, C. van, and E. de Jonghe. Les Mayombe. Brussels, 1907.

Weyns, J. A. Drie merkwaardige Schepters nit Neder Kongo, *Bulletin des Musées Royaux (Belge) d'Art et d'Histoire*, III (1943), 44–48.

—— Un Chef-d'Œuvre de la sculpture africaine provenant des Bakongo Occidentaux, *Bulletin des Musées Royaux (Belge) d'Art et d'Histoire*, III (1944), 71–82.

—— Een afrikaansch Beeld van een Buktenaar, *Bulletin des Musées Royaux (Belge) d'Art et d'Histoire*, III (1945). 76–80.

WESTERN CONGO

Einstein, C. Masques Bapendé, *Documents,* I (1930), 48–54.
Guiral, L. Les Batékés, Afrique Occidentale, *Revue d'Ethnographie,* V (1886), 134–166.
Plancquaert, M. Sociétés Secrètes Bayaka. Brussels, 1930.
—— Les Jaga et les Bayaka du Kwango. Brussels, 1932.
Torday, E., and T. A. Joyce. Notes on the Ethnography of the Bayaka, *Journal of the Royal Anthropological Institute,* XXXVI (1906), 39–59.

CENTRAL CONGO

Annales du Musee du Congo Belge (*Tervuren*). Les Arts. *Religion, Ethnographie et Anthropologie,* III (Brussels), 1902–1906.
Bevel, M. L. L'Art de la décoration chez les Basonge. *Conseiller Congolaise,* X (1937), 1, 10.
Clouzot, H., and A. Level. L'Art du Congo Belge, *Art et Décoration,* XL (1921), 149–160.
Joyce, T. A. On a Wooden Portrait Statue from the Bushongo People of the Kasai District, Congo State, *Man,* X (1910), 1–2.
—— Babunda Weaving, *Ipek,* I (1925), 105–110.
—— The Portrait Statue of Mikobe-Mbula, 110th Paramount Chief of the Bushongo, *Man,* XXV (1925), 185–186.
Maes, J. La Sculpture Bashilele, *Cahier Belgique,* VI (1928), 238.
—— Le Tissage chez populations du Lac Leopold II, *Anthropos,* XXV (1930), 393–408.
—— Les Statues de rois Bakuba, *Beaux-Arts,* VII (1936), 18–21.
Overbergh, C. van. Les Basonge, Brussels, 1908.
Pierpont, J. de. Les Bambala, *Congo,* I (1932), 22–37; 185–205.
Soupault, P. L'Art nègre au Congo, *Le Miroir du Congo Belge,* II (1929), 203–250.
Torday, E. Camp and Tramp in African Wilds. London, 1913.
—— On the Trail of the Bushongo. Philadelphia, 1925.
Torday, E., and T. A. Joyce. Notes on the Ethnography of the Bambala, *Journal of the Royal Anthropological Institute,* XXXV (1905), 398–426.
—— Les Bushongo, *Annales du Musèe du Congo Belge (Tervuren),* Series IV. Brussels, 1910. Vol. II.
Vervaecke, R. P. Les Bena Lulua, *Revue Congo,* 1910.

EASTERN CONGO

Burton, W. F. P. The Country of the Baluba in Central Katanga, *Geographical Journal,* LXX (1927), 321–342.
Burton, W. F. P. The Secret Societies of Lubaland, Congo Belge, *Bantu Studies,* IV (1930), 217–250.

Colle, R. P. Les Baluba Hemba. Brussels, 1913.
—— Les Baluba. Brussels, 1913.
Delhaise, C. Les Warega. Brussels, 1909.
Maes, J. Notes sur le matériel du feticheur Baluba, *Man*, XI
(1911), 181–185.
—— Les Appuis-tête du Congo Belge, *Annales du Musée du
Congo Belge (Tervuren)*, Series, VI (1929), Vol. I, 1–44.
—— Les Trépieds et appuis-dos du Congo Belge, *Annales du
Musée du Congo Belge (Tervuren)*, Series, VI (1930), Vol. I,
45–78.
—— L'Ethnologie de l'Afrique Centrale et le Musée du Congo
Belge, *Africa*, VII (1934), 174–190.
—— Kabila en Grafbeelden uit Kongo, *Annales du Musée du
Congo Belge (Tervuren)*, Series, VI (1938), Vol. II, 1–64.
——Les Kabila ou figures mendiantes, *Annales du Musée du
Congo Belge (Tervuren)*, Series, VI (1938), 65–148.
—— Moedereerebeelden uit Kongo, *Annales du Musée du
Congo Belge (Tervuren)*, Series, VI (1939), Vol. II, 149 ff.
Olbrechts, Frans M. De Kabila Stijl, *Wetensch Tijdingen*, V
(1940), 22–30.

SOUTHERN CONGO

Barns, T. A. Angolan Sketches. London, 1928.
Baumann, H. Lunda. Berlin, 1935.
Correia, P. J. Une Étude de l'ethnographie d'Angola, *An-
thropos*, XX (1925), 325–331.
Homburger, L. Angola et Rodesia, Mission Rohan-Chabot.
Paris, 1925.
Monard, A. Notes sur les collections ethnographiques de la
Mission Scientifique Suisse en Angola, 1928–29, *Bulletin de
la Société Neuchâteloise de Geographie*, XXXIX (1930), 100–
122.
Nairn, M. Congo Art. *Studio*, CXXX (1945), 88–89.

NORTHERN CONGO

Baumann, H. Die materielle Kultur der Azande und Mang-
betu, *Baessler-archiv*, XI (1927), 1–131.
Birnbaum, M. The Long-headed Mangbetu, *Natural History*,
XLIII (1939), 73–83.
Clouzot, H. Les Arts appliques Mangbetu, *La Renaissance*, IX
(1926), 569–572.
Kerken, G. van der. Notes sur les Mangbetu. Antwerp, 1932.
Lagal, C. R. Les Azande ou Niam-Niam. Brussels, 1926.
Lang, H. Famous Ivory Treasures of a Negro King, *Journal of
the American Museum of Natural History*, XVIII (1918),
527–552.

Overbergh, G. van, and E. de Jonghe. Les Bangala. Brussels, 1907.
—— Les Mangbetu. Brussels, 1909.

EAST AFRICA

Collings, H. D. Notes on the Makonde Tribe of Portuguese East Africa, *Man*, XXIX (1929), 25–28.

Joyce, T. A. On a Ceremonial Mask and Dress from the Upper Zambesi, Now in the British Museum, *Man*, III (1903), 75.

Marwick, B. A. The Swazi; an Ethnographic Account. Cambridge, 1940.

Sharpe, A. A Carved Stool and Other Objects from British East Africa, *Man*, I (1901), 49.

PLATES

1   SEATED FEMALE
FIGURE, WOOD, 20 7/8
INCHES HIGH
BAMBARA STYLE, SUDAN
UNIVERSITY MUSEUM
PHILADELPHIA (AF 5365)

2   TWIN FIGURE, WOOD
CA. 9 INCHES HIGH
BAMBARA STYLE (?), SUDAN
BROOKLYN MUSEUM (22.1456)

3   SIDE VIEW OF FIGURE 2

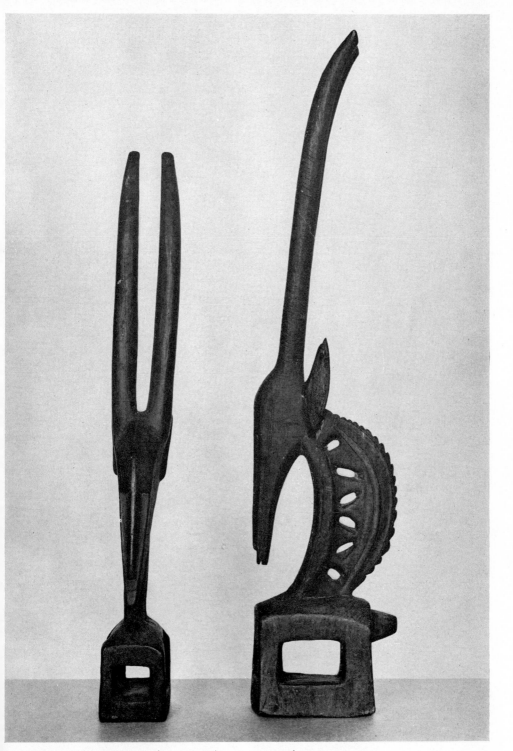

4 ANTELOPE HEADPIECE (TJI WARA), WOOD, 24¾ INCHES HIGH
BAMBARA STYLE, SUDAN
UNIVERSITY MUSEUM, PHILADELPHIA (29–12–125)

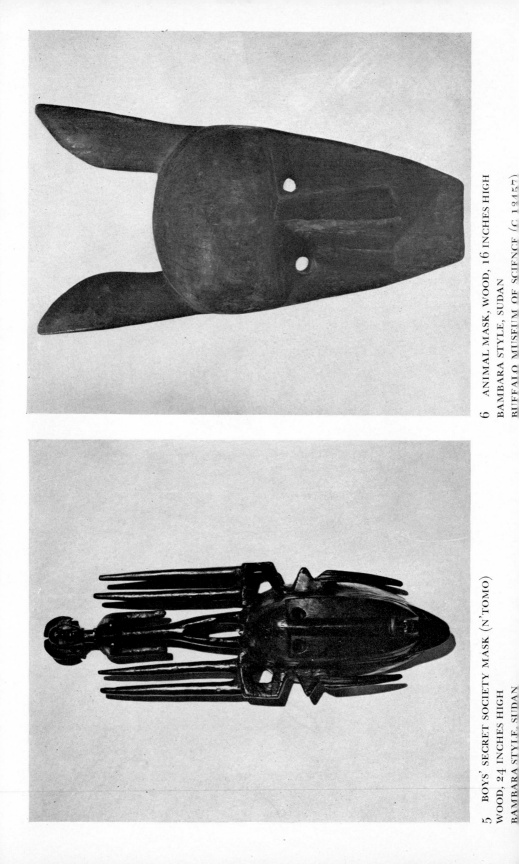

6 ANIMAL MASK, WOOD, 16 INCHES HIGH
BAMBARA STYLE, SUDAN
BUFFALO MUSEUM OF SCIENCE (C 1347)

5 BOYS' SECRET SOCIETY MASK (N'TOMO)
WOOD, 24 INCHES HIGH
BAMBARA STYLE, SUDAN

7   SEATED FIGURE
WOOD, 22⅘ INCHES
HIGH
DOGON STYLE
SUDAN
UNIVERSITY MUSEUM
PHILADELPHIA
(29–12–97)

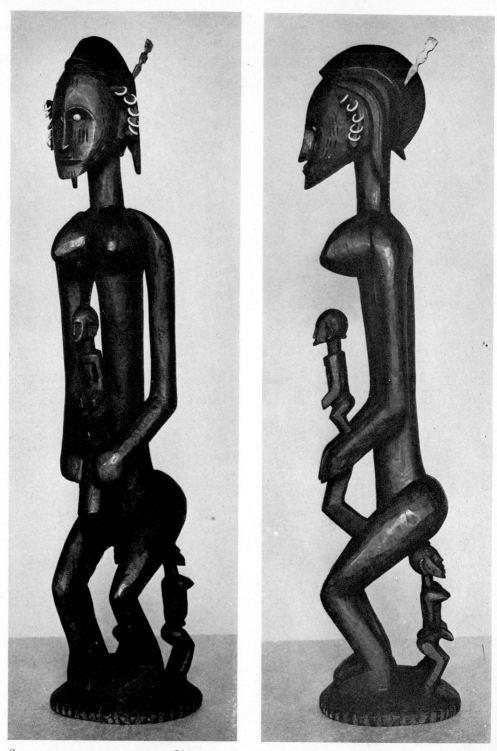

8   SEATED FIGURE, WOOD, 21⅗ INCHES HIGH
DOGON STYLE (BANDIAGARA), SUDAN
UNIVERSITY MUSEUM, PHILADELPHIA (29–12–98)

9   STANDING MALE
FIGURE, WOOD, 26½
INCHES HIGH
BAGA STYLE, FRENCH
GUINEA
BUFFALO MUSEUM OF
SCIENCE (C 13146)

10   FEMALE SECRET SOCIETY MASK (BUNDU), WOOD, 14 INCHES HIGH
MENDI STYLE, SIERRA LEONE
BUFFALO MUSEUM OF SCIENCE (C 12978)

11   STAFF USED BY FEMALE SECRET SOCIETY, WOOD, 30 INCHES HIGH
MENDI STYLE, SIERRA LEONE
UNIVERSITY MUSEUM, PHILADELPHIA (37–22–3)

12   DIVINATION FIGURE (YASSI), WOOD, 17½ INCHES HIGH
MENDI STYLE (SHERBRO), SIERRA LEONE
UNIVERSITY MUSEUM, PHILADELPHIA (37-22-279)

13 SECRET SOCIETY
MASK (PORO), WOOD
22 INCHES HIGH
MANO TRIBE, LIBERIA
PEABODY MUSEUM
HARVARD UNIVERSITY
(37–77–50/2744)

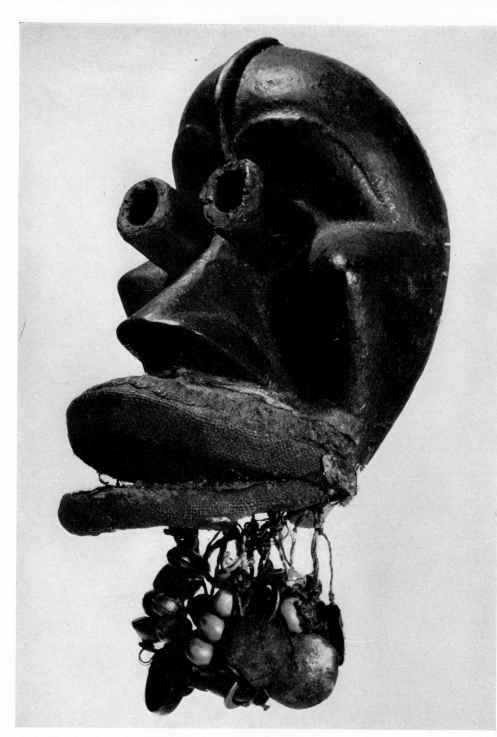

14 SECRET SOCIETY MASK (PORO), WOOD, HINGED JAWS COVERED WITH CLOTH
SEEDS SUSPENDED BENEATH JAW, 10 INCHES HIGH
GEH TRIBE (?), LIBERIA
PEABODY MUSEUM, HARVARD UNIVERSITY (40–34–50/4588)

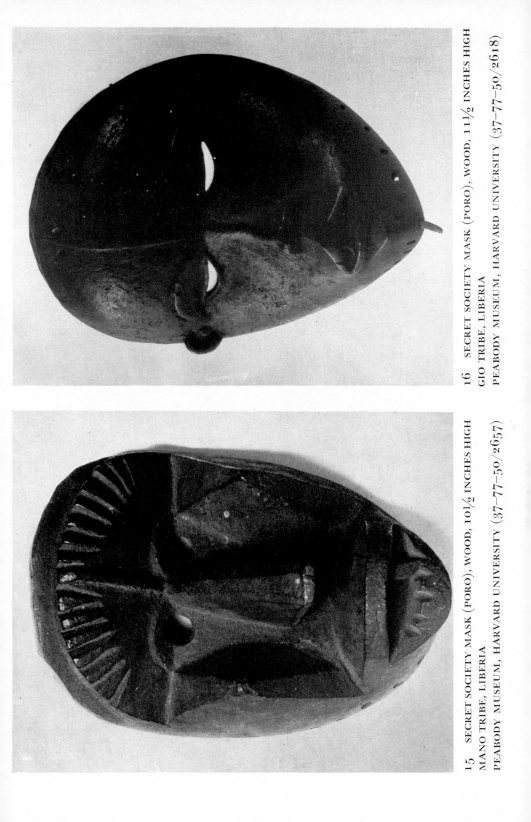

15　SECRET SOCIETY MASK (PORO), WOOD, 10½ INCHES HIGH
MANO TRIBE, LIBERIA
PEABODY MUSEUM, HARVARD UNIVERSITY (37–77–50/2657)

16　SECRET SOCIETY MASK (PORO), WOOD, 11½ INCHES HIGH
GIO TRIBE, LIBERIA
PEABODY MUSEUM, HARVARD UNIVERSITY (37–77–50/2618)

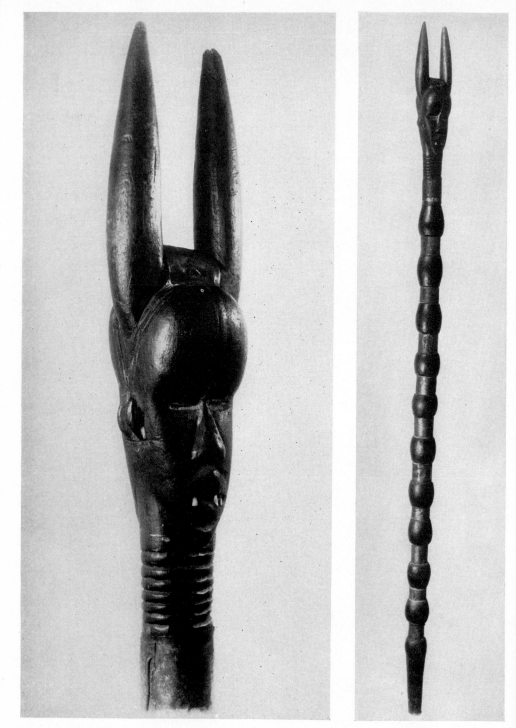

17   STAFF USED BY SECRET SOCIETY (PORO), WOOD, METAL DETAIL, 4½ FEET HIGH
MANO TRIBE (?), LIBERIA
PEABODY MUSEUM, HARVARD UNIVERSITY (L/279)

18   STANDING FEMALE
FIGURE, WOOD
20¼ INCHES HIGH
BAOULÉ STYLE
IVORY COAST
AMERICAN MUSEUM OF
NATURAL HISTORY
NEW YORK (90.1/6994)

19 SEATED FEMALE
FIGURE, WOOD
22 INCHES HIGH
BAOULÉ STYLE
IVORY COAST
COLLECTION VINCENT
PRICE, BEVERLY HILLS

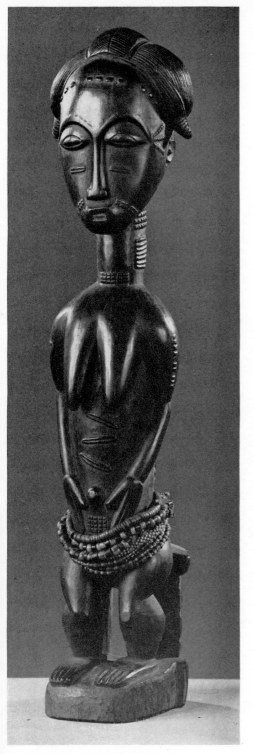

20 SEATED FEMALE FIGURE
WOOD, 17 INCHES HIGH
BAOULÉ STYLE, IVORY COAST
UNIVERSITY MUSEUM, PHILADELPHIA
(29–12–69)

21 STANDING MALE FIGURE, WOOD, 16¼
INCHES HIGH. BAOULÉ STYLE, IVORY COAST
UNIVERSITY MUSEUM, PHILADELPHIA
(29–12–72)

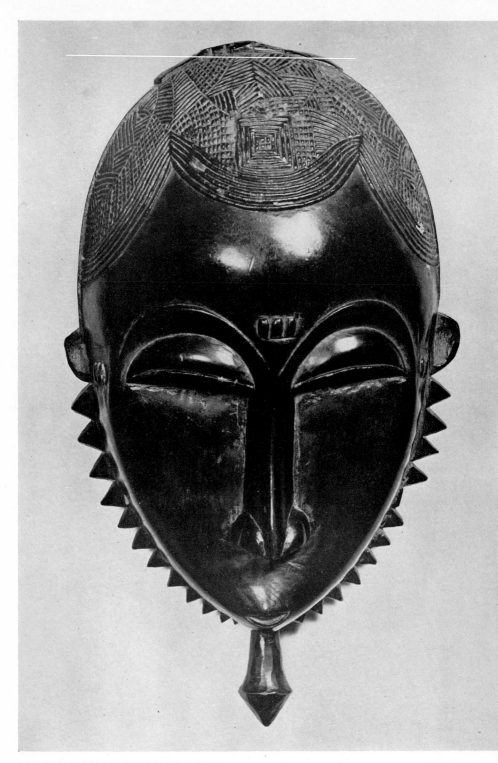

22   MASK, WOOD, 15 INCHES HIGH
BAOULÉ STYLE, IVORY COAST
BUFFALO MUSEUM OF SCIENCE (C 12719)

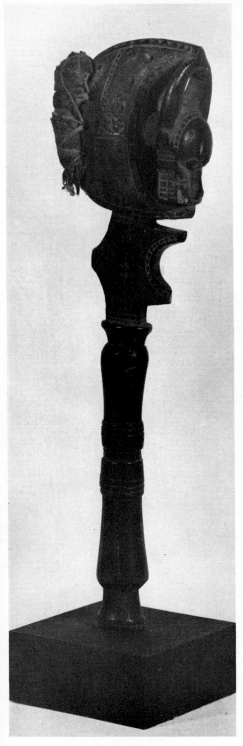

23 GONG MALLET, WOOD
9 INCHES HIGH
BAOULÉ STYLE, IVORY COAST
BUFFALO MUSEUM OF SCIENCE (C 12515)

24 STANDING MALE FIGURE, WOOD, 16½
INCHES HIGH. GURO STYLE, IVORY COAST
UNIVERSITY MUSEUM, PHILADELPHIA
(29-12-81)

25 HORNED MASK WITH BIRD, WOOD, 20½ INCHE HIGH OVER-ALL. GURO STYLE (?), IVORY COAST UNIVERSITY MUSEUM PHILADELPHIA (29–35–1)

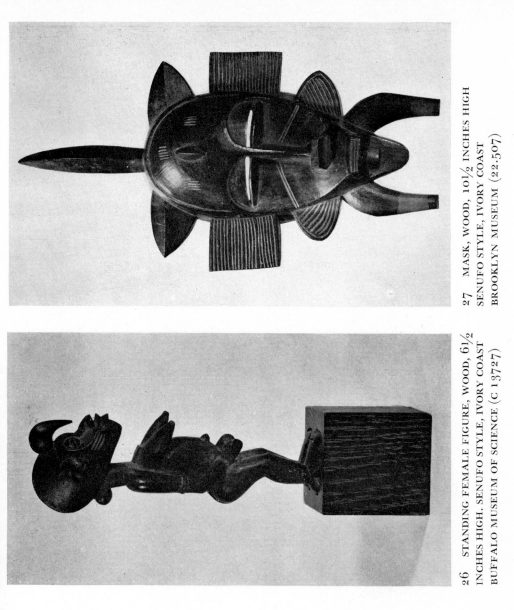

27 MASK, WOOD, 10½ INCHES HIGH
SENUFO STYLE, IVORY COAST
BROOKLYN MUSEUM (22.507)

26 STANDING FEMALE FIGURE, WOOD, 6½
INCHES HIGH. SENUFO STYLE, IVORY COAST
BUFFALO MUSEUM OF SCIENCE (C 13727)

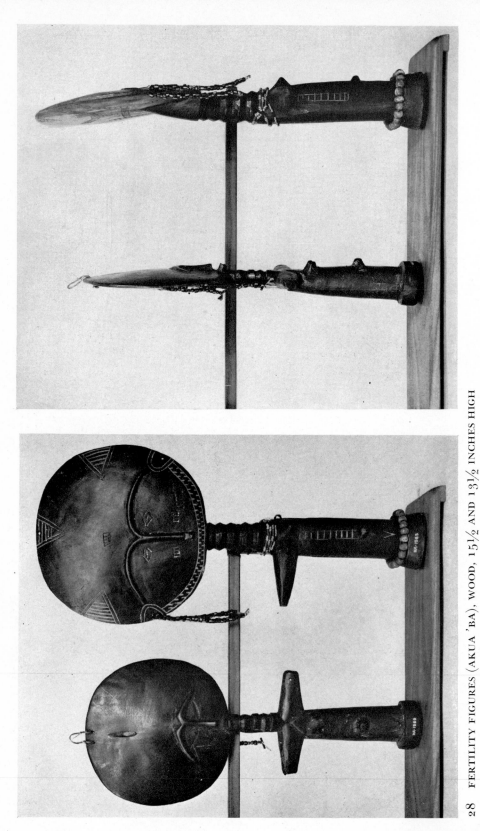

28 FERTILITY FIGURES (AKUA 'BA), WOOD, 15½ AND 13½ INCHES HIGH
ASHANTI STYLE, GOLD COAST
ROYAL ONTARIO MUSEUM OF ARCHAEOLOGY, TORONTO (HA 1965 · HA 1968)

29   GOLD WEIGHTS, BRONZE, CAST BY CIRE PERDU (LOST WAX) PROCESS. DEPICTING
PROVERBS, FANTASTIC ANIMALS, AND SCENES FROM DAILY LIFE, 1-2½ INCHES HIGH
ASHANTI STYLE, GOLD COAST
UNIVERSITY MUSEUM, PHILADELPHIA; BUFFALO MUSEUM OF SCIENCE

30   URN (KUDUO), BRONZE, 8¾ INCHES HIGH
ASHANTI STYLE, GOLD COAST
COLLECTION WILLIAM MOORE, LOS ANGELES

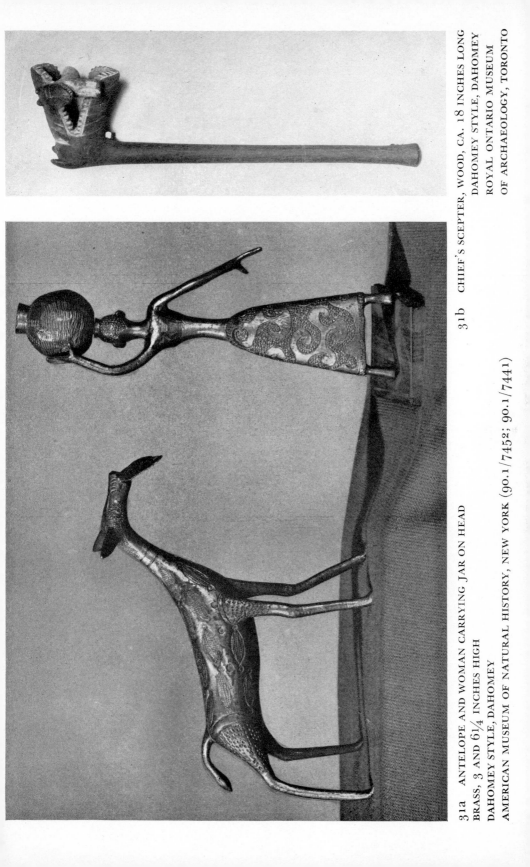

31a   ANTELOPE AND WOMAN CARRYING JAR ON HEAD
BRASS, 3 AND 6¼ INCHES HIGH
DAHOMEY STYLE, DAHOMEY
AMERICAN MUSEUM OF NATURAL HISTORY, NEW YORK (90.1/7452; 90.1/7441)

31b   CHIEF'S SCEPTER, WOOD, CA. 18 INCHES LONG
DAHOMEY STYLE, DAHOMEY
ROYAL ONTARIO MUSEUM
OF ARCHAEOLOGY, TORONTO

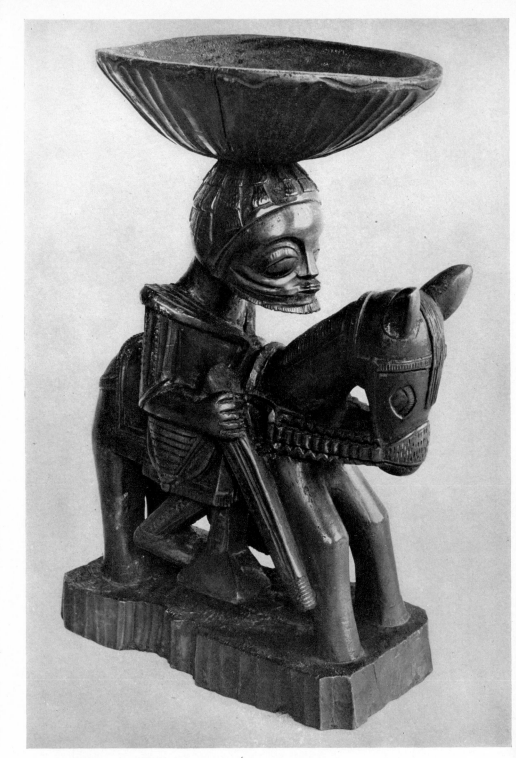

32   EQUESTRIAN FIGURE, WOOD, 11¾ INCHES HIGH
YORUBA STYLE, NIGERIA
NEWARK MUSEUM (24.2458)

33   TWIN FIGURES, WOOD, 8¾ AND CA. 9 INCHES HIGH
YORUBA STYLE, NIGERIA
BUFFALO MUSEUM OF SCIENCE (C 12975)
ROYAL ONTARIO MUSEUM OF ARCHAEOLOGY, TORONTO (HA. 872)

34   STAFF SUPPORTING MOTHER AND CHILD, WOOD, 15 INCHES HIGH
YORUBA STYLE, NIGERIA
COLLECTION RENE D'HARNONCOURT, NEW YORK

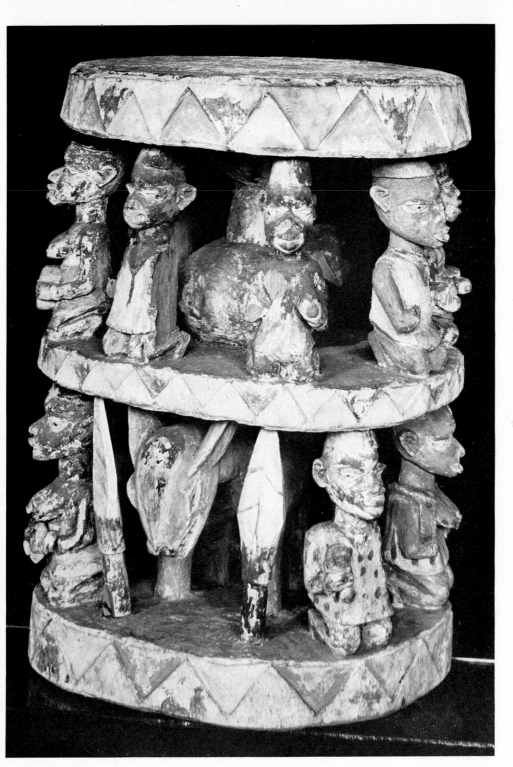

35   STOOL WITH TWO TIERS OF FIGURES, POLYCHROMED WOOD, CA. 30 INCHES HIGH
YORUBA STYLE, NIGERIA
ROYAL ONTARIO MUSEUM OF ARCHAEOLOGY, TORONTO

36 DIVINATION VESSEL, POLYCHROMED WOOD, 25 INCHES HIGH
YORUBA STYLE, NIGERIA
COLLECTION WILLIAM MOORE, LOS ANGELES

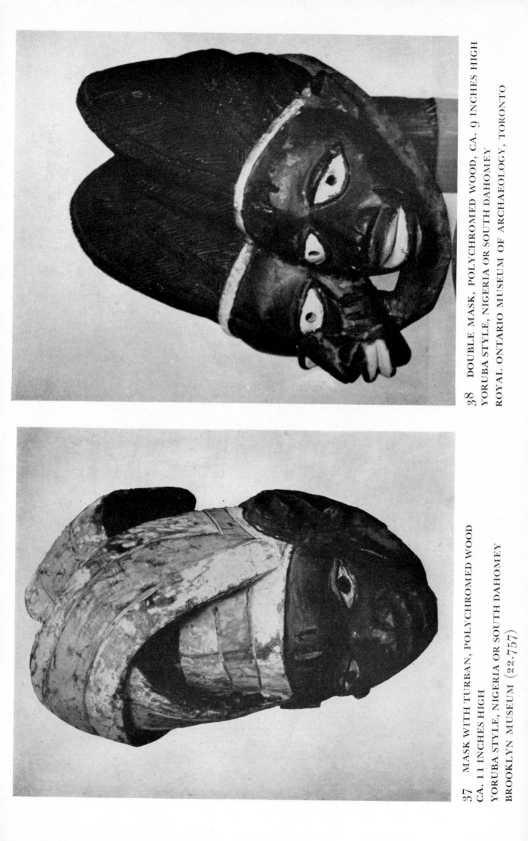

38   DOUBLE MASK, POLYCHROMED WOOD, CA. 9 INCHES HIGH
YORUBA STYLE, NIGERIA OR SOUTH DAHOMEY
ROYAL ONTARIO MUSEUM OF ARCHAEOLOGY, TORONTO

37   MASK WITH TURBAN, POLYCHROMED WOOD
CA. 11 INCHES HIGH
YORUBA STYLE, NIGERIA OR SOUTH DAHOMEY
BROOKLYN MUSEUM (22·757)

39   LARGE MASK WITH CARVED GROUP, POLYCHROMED WOOD, 39 INCHES HIGH
YORUBA STYLE, NIGERIA
UNIVERSITY MUSEUM, PHILADELPHIA (AF 2002)

40   MALE AND FEMALE HEADS, BRONZE, 12½ AND 9¾ INCHES HIGH
IFÉ STYLE, NIGERIA
COLLECTION PROFESSOR WILLIAM R. BASCOM, EVANSTON, ILL.

41   ALTAR HEAD OF KING, BRONZE, 17½ INCHES HIGH
BENIN STYLE, NIGERIA
UNIVERSITY MUSEUM, PHILADELPHIA (AF 5081)

42   RELIEF PLAQUE WITH THREE FIGURES, BRONZE
CA. 20 INCHES HIGH, 18 INCHES WIDE
BENIN STYLE, NIGERIA
UNIVERSITY MUSEUM, PHILADELPHIA (AF 2066)

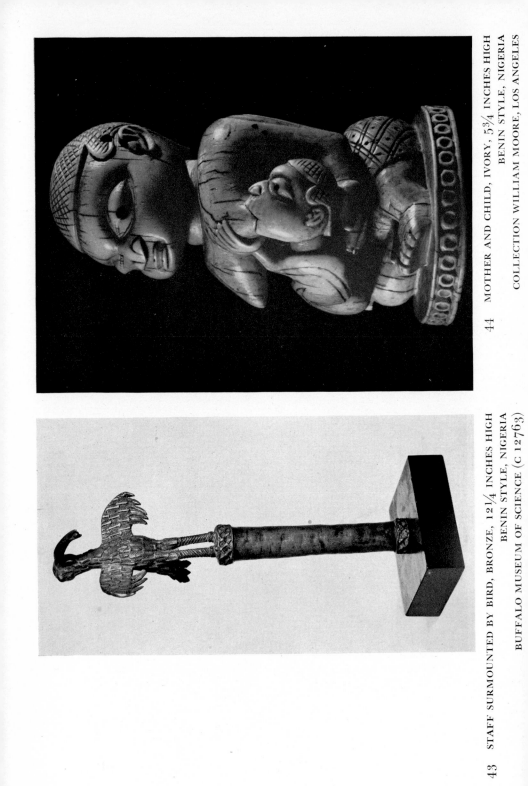

43 STAFF SURMOUNTED BY BIRD, BRONZE, 12¼ INCHES HIGH
BENIN STYLE, NIGERIA
BUFFALO MUSEUM OF SCIENCE (C 12763)

44 MOTHER AND CHILD, IVORY, 5¾ INCHES HIGH
BENIN STYLE, NIGERIA
COLLECTION WILLIAM MOORE, LOS ANGELES

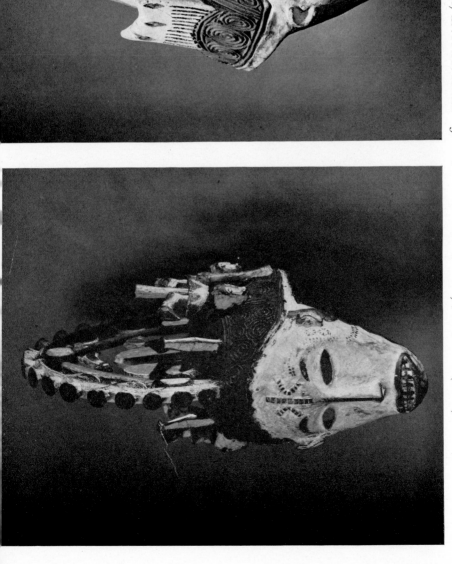

45 FUNERARY MASK (MAW), WOOD, 17½ INCHES HIGH
IBO STYLE, NIGERIA
UNIVERSITY MUSEUM, PHILADELPHIA (AF 5371)

46 FUNERARY MASK (MAW), WOOD, 16½ INCHES HIGH
IBO STYLE, NIGERIA
AMERICAN MUSEUM OF NATURAL HISTORY, NEW YORK (90.1/7587)

47   SEATED FEMALE
FIGURE, MASK TOP, WOO~
24 INCHES HIGH
IBIBIO STYLE, NIGERIA
COLLECTION DR. RALPH
LINTON, NEW HAVEN
CONN.

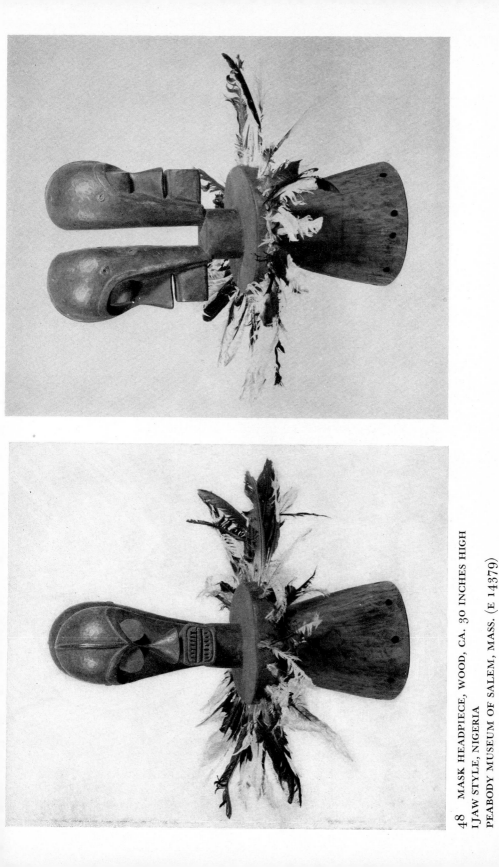

48 MASK HEADPIECE, WOOD, CA. 30 INCHES HIGH
IJAW STYLE, NIGERIA
PEABODY MUSEUM OF SALEM, MASS. (E 14379)

49 MASK, WOOD
CA. 14 INCHES HIGH
IJAW STYLE, NIGERIA
PEABODY MUSEUM OF
SALEM, MASS. (E 6764)

50   SKIN-COVERED HEAD WORN AS MASK HEADPIECE, ANIMAL SKIN OVER
PALMWOOD FRAME, 9 INCHES HIGH
EKOI STYLE, NIGERIA—SOUTHWEST CAMEROON
BUFFALO MUSEUM OF SCIENCE (C 13147)

51 STANDING FIGURE
WOOD, 15½ INCHES
HIGH
CAMEROON STYLE
CENTRAL CAMEROON
CHICAGO NATURAL
HISTORY MUSEUM
(175691)

52 SEATED FIGURE
HOLDING BOWL, WOOD
16¼ INCHES HIGH
CAMEROON STYLE
CENTRAL CAMEROON
BUFFALO MUSEUM OF
SCIENCE (C 12516)

53   STANDING FIGURE, WOOD
CA. 20 INCHES HIGH. CAMEROON STYLE
CENTRAL CAMEROON
PEABODY MUSEUM, HARVARD UNIVERSITY
(B 4959)

54   STANDING FIGURE, WOOD, 18 INCHES
HIGH. CAMEROON STYLE
CENTRAL CAMEROON
PEABODY MUSEUM, HARVARD UNIVERSITY
(B 4931)

55 BOWL SUPPORTED BY CARVED ANIMALS
WOOD, 10½ INCHES HIGH
CAMEROON STYLE, CENTRAL CAMEROON
BUFFALO MUSEUM OF SCIENCE (C 1303g)

56 STOOL SUPPORTED BY CARVED ANIMALS, WOOD WITH BEADED SURFACE
16 INCHES HIGH, 17 INCHES DIAMETER
CAMEROON STYLE, CENTRAL CAMEROON
CHICAGO NATURAL HISTORY MUSEUM (175559)

57   DOOR LINTEL CARVED WITH ANIMALS, WOOD, 41 INCHES LONG, 7 INCHES HIGH
CAMEROON STYLE, CENTRAL CAMEROON
BUFFALO MUSEUM OF SCIENCE (C 13040)

58   LARGE ANIMAL MASK, WOOD, 13 INCHES HIGH
CAMEROON STYLE, CENTRAL CAMEROON
BUFFALO MUSEUM OF SCIENCE (C 13037)

59   LARGE ANIMAL MASK, WOOD, 18 INCHES HIGH
CAMEROON STYLE, CENTRAL CAMEROON
COLLECTION DR. RALPH LINTON, NEW HAVEN, CONN.

60   MASK, BRASS, 12 INCHES HIGH
CAMEROON STYLE, CENTRAL CAMEROON
AMERICAN MUSEUM OF NATURAL HISTORY (90.1/7488)

61   STAFF SURMOUNTED BY HUMAN FIGURE AND ANIMAL
BRASS, FIGURE 10 INCHES HIGH
CAMEROON STYLE, CENTRAL CAMEROON
PEABODY MUSEUM, HARVARD UNIVERSITY

62   PIPE BOWL, SEATED FIGURE, BLACK CLAY, 8 INCHES HIGH
CAMEROON STYLE, CENTRAL CAMEROON
CHICAGO NATURAL HISTORY MUSEUM (174983)

63   SEATED MALE
FIGURE, WOOD,
23½ INCHES HIGH
FANG STYLE, CAMEROON
GABUN
PEABODY MUSEUM
HARVARD UNIVERSITY
(B 2132)

64   SEATED MALE FIGURE, WOOD, 24 INCHES HIGH
FANG STYLE, SOUTHEAST CAMEROON-GABUN
PEABODY MUSEUM, HARVARD UNIVERSITY (B 3822)

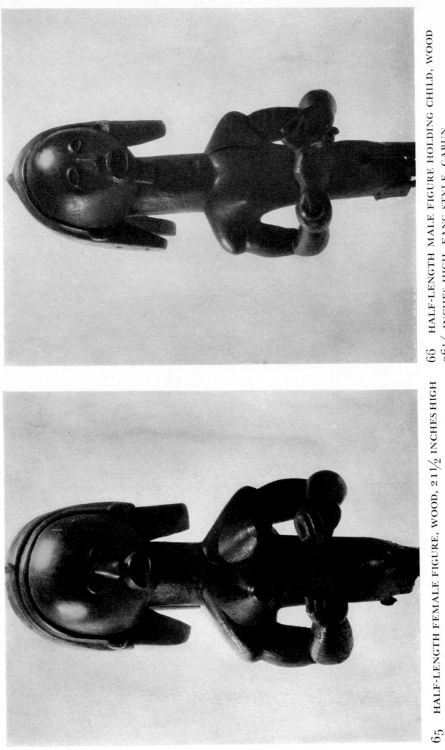

65 HALF-LENGTH FEMALE FIGURE, WOOD, 211/2 INCHES HIGH
FANG STYLE, GABUN
PEABODY MUSEUM, HARVARD UNIVERSITY (B 4973)

66 HALF-LENGTH MALE FIGURE HOLDING CHILD, WOOD
261/2 INCHES HIGH. FANG STYLE, GABUN
PEABODY MUSEUM, HARVARD UNIVERSITY (B 4974)

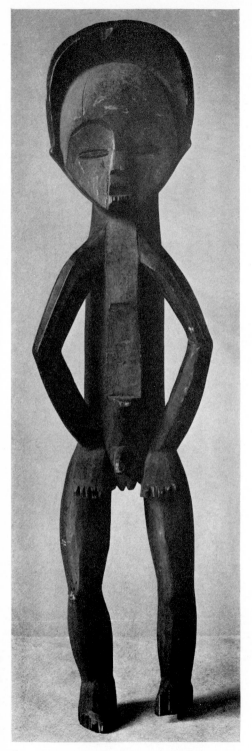 

67   STANDING MALE FIGURE, WOOD
30 INCHES HIGH
FANG STYLE, GABUN
UNIVERSITY MUSEUM, PHILADELPHIA
(AF 5188)

68   THREE-QUARTER PROFILE VIEW OF
FIGURE 67.

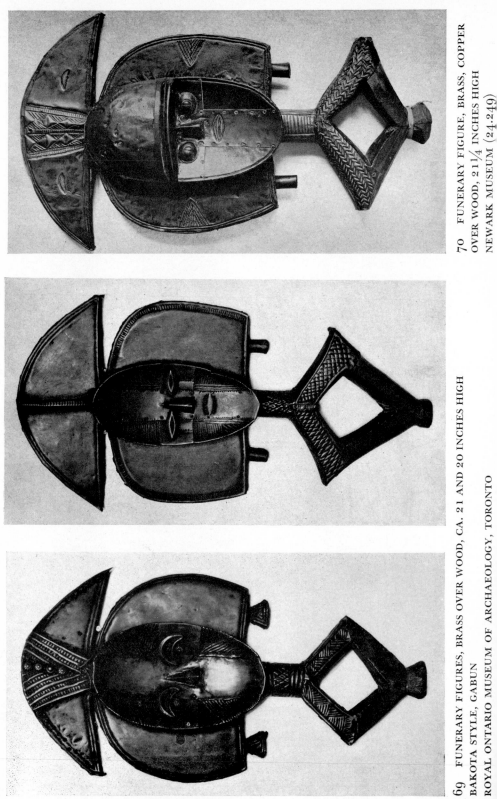

70 FUNERARY FIGURE, BRASS, COPPER
OVER WOOD, 21¼ INCHES HIGH
NEWARK MUSEUM (24.249)

69 FUNERARY FIGURES, BRASS OVER WOOD, CA. 21 AND 20 INCHES HIGH
BAKOTA STYLE, GABUN
ROYAL ONTARIO MUSEUM OF ARCHAEOLOGY, TORONTO

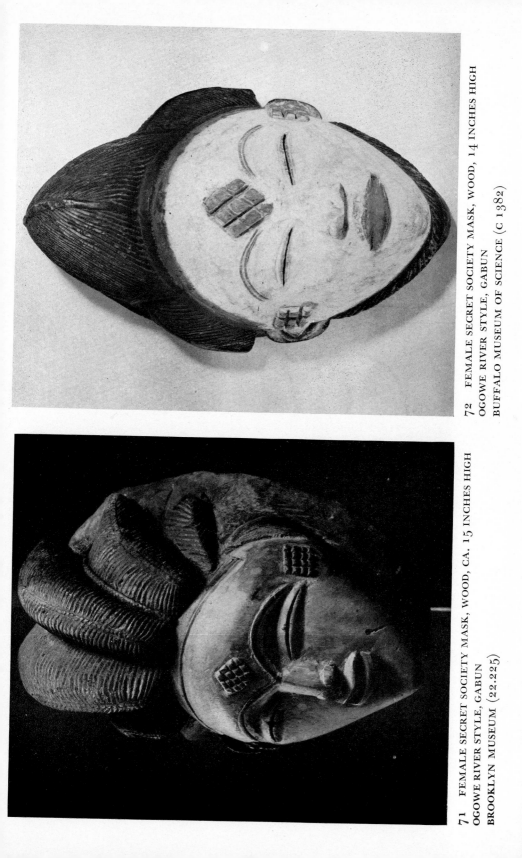

72 FEMALE SECRET SOCIETY MASK, WOOD, 14 INCHES HIGH
OGOWE RIVER STYLE, GABUN
BUFFALO MUSEUM OF SCIENCE (C 1382)

71 FEMALE SECRET SOCIETY MASK, WOOD, CA. 15 INCHES HIGH
OGOWE RIVER STYLE, GABUN
BROOKLYN MUSEUM (22.225)

73   KNEELING FEMALE FIGURE, WOOD, 11½ INCHES HIGH
LOWER CONGO STYLE, WESTERN BELGIAN CONGO
AMERICAN MUSEUM OF NATURAL HISTORY, NEW YORK (90.1/5898)

74   KNEELING FEMALE FETISH FIGURE, WOOD, 12 INCHES HIGH
LOWER CONGO STYLE, WESTERN BELGIAN CONGO
PEABODY MUSEUM, HARVARD UNIVERSITY (B 1582)

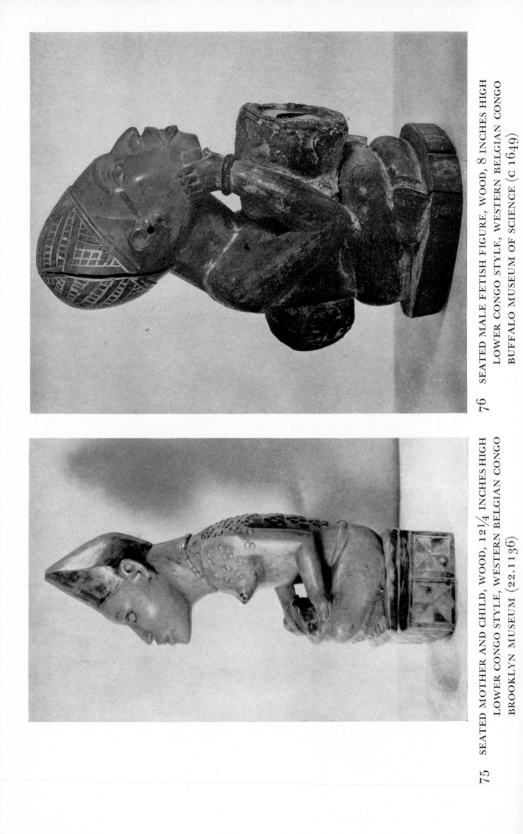

75 SEATED MOTHER AND CHILD, WOOD, 12¼ INCHES HIGH
LOWER CONGO STYLE, WESTERN BELGIAN CONGO
BROOKLYN MUSEUM (22.1136)

76 SEATED MALE FETISH FIGURE, WOOD, 8 INCHES HIGH
LOWER CONGO STYLE, WESTERN BELGIAN CONGO
BUFFALO MUSEUM OF SCIENCE (C 1649)

77 STANDING MALE
FETISH FIGURE, WOOD
12½ INCHES HIGH
BATEKE STYLE
WESTERN BELGIAN
CONGO
UNIVERSITY MUSEUM
PHILADELPHIA (AF 4706)

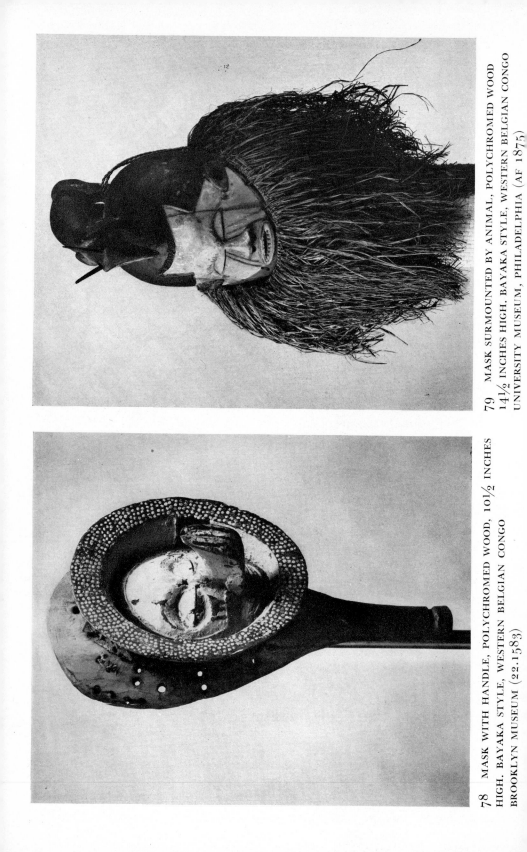

78 MASK WITH HANDLE, POLYCHROMED WOOD, 10½ INCHES HIGH. BAYAKA STYLE, WESTERN BELGIAN CONGO BROOKLYN MUSEUM (22.1583)

79 MASK SURMOUNTED BY ANIMAL, POLYCHROMED WOOD 14½ INCHES HIGH. BAYAKA STYLE, WESTERN BELGIAN CONGO UNIVERSITY MUSEUM, PHILADELPHIA (AF 1875)

80 STANDING FEMALE FIGURE, WOOD, 11 INCHES HIGH
BAYAKA STYLE, WESTERN BELGIAN CONGO
PEABODY MUSEUM, HARVARD UNIVERSITY (B 1554)

81 VERTICAL DRUM
CARVED WITH HEAD
WOOD, CA. 14 INCHES
HIGH
BAYAKA STYLE
WESTERN BELGIAN
CONGO
COLLECTION CHARLES
B. SPENCER, JR.
NEW YORK

82 NECK-REST AND WHISTLE, WOOD, 5½ AND 6 INCHES HIGH
BAYAKA STYLE, WESTERN BELGIAN CONGO
BUFFALO MUSEUM OF SCIENCE (C 12781; C 12622)

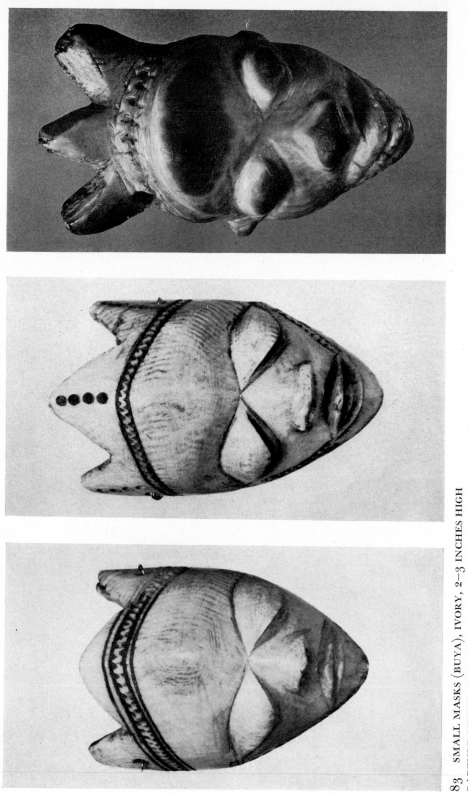

83   SMALL MASKS (BUYA), IVORY, 2–3 INCHES HIGH
BAPENDE STYLE, WEST CENTRAL BELGIAN CONGO
BROOKLYN MUSEUM; UNIVERSITY MUSEUM, PHILADELPHIA (30–59–1)

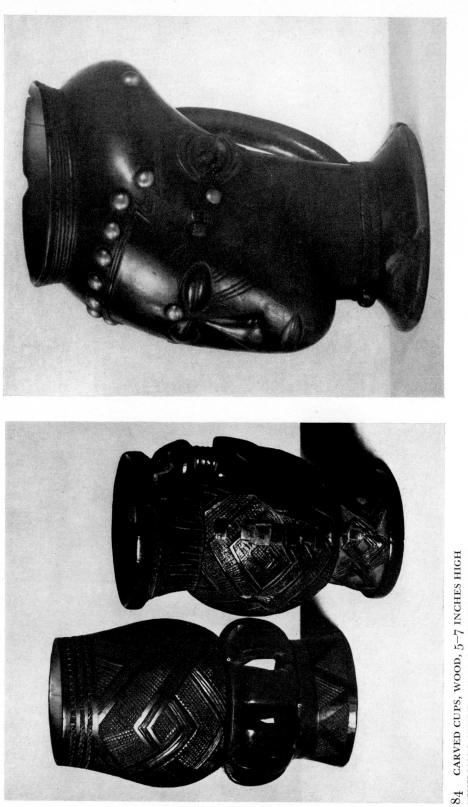

84 CARVED CUPS, WOOD, 5–7 INCHES HIGH
BUSHONGO STYLE, CENTRAL BELGIAN CONGO
BUFFALO MUSEUM OF SCIENCE (C 12700; C 12769); BROOKLYN MUSEUM (22.1487)

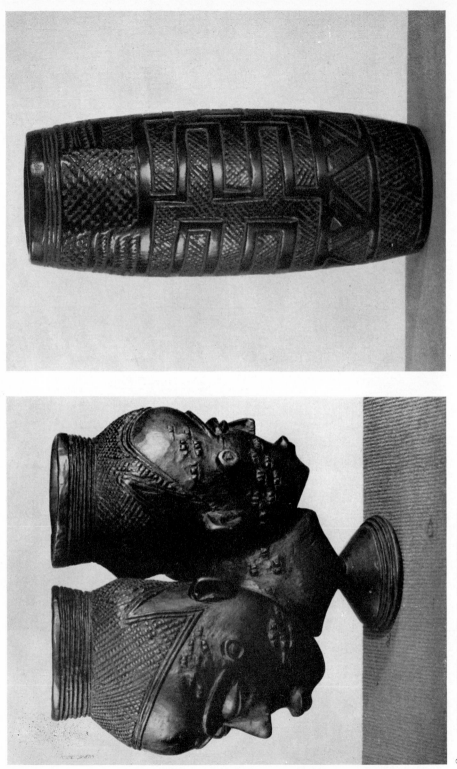

85   CARVED CUPS, WOOD, 5–7 INCHES HIGH
BUSHONGO STYLE, CENTRAL BELGIAN CONGO
BROOKLYN MUSEUM (22.1488; 22.173)

86   CARVED BOX, WOOD, 7½ INCHES LONG, 3¼ INCHES HIGH
BUSHONGO STYLE, CENTRAL BELGIAN CONGO
BUFFALO MUSEUM OF SCIENCE (C 12697)

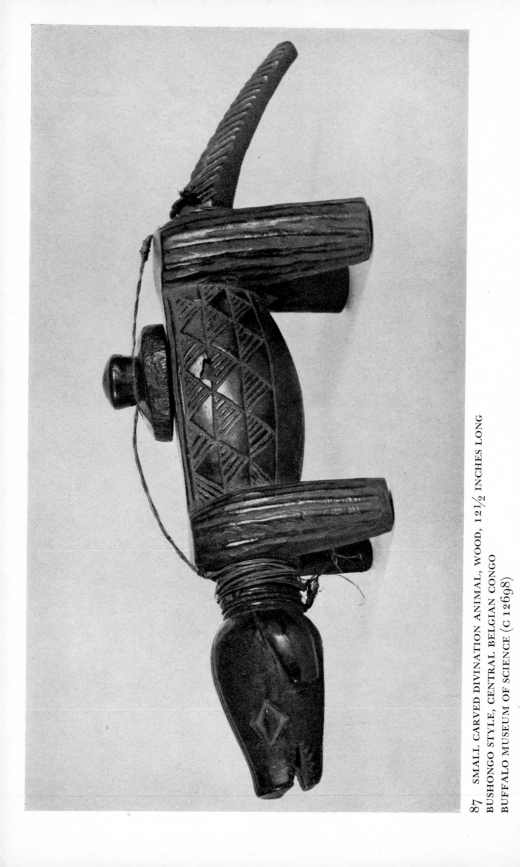

87 SMALL CARVED DIVINATION ANIMAL, WOOD, 12½ INCHES LONG
BUSHONGO STYLE, CENTRAL BELGIAN CONGO
BUFFALO MUSEUM OF SCIENCE (C 12698)

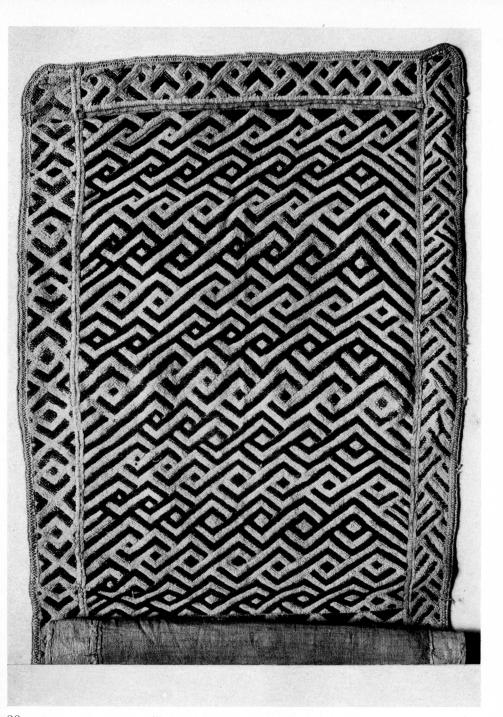

88   RAFFIA PILE CLOTH ("VELVET"), 51 INCHES BY 24 INCHES
BUSHONGO STYLE, CENTRAL BELGIAN CONGO
UNIVERSITY MUSEUM, PHILADELPHIA (AF 1416)

89 CARVED DRUMS, WOOD, 27½ AND 24¼ INCHES HIGH
BUSHONGO STYLE, CENTRAL BELGIAN CONGO
ROYAL ONTARIO MUSEUM OF ARCHAEOLOGY, TORONTO (HAC.395; HAC.397)

90　STANDING MALE FIGURE, WOOD, 9½ INCHES HIGH
BENA LULUA STYLE, CENTRAL BELGIAN CONGO
UNIVERSITY MUSEUM, PHILADELPHIA (AF 628)

91　SQUATTING FETISH FIGURE AND STANDING FETISH FIGURE
WOOD, 5 AND 7 INCHES HIGH
BENA LULUA STYLE, CENTRAL BELGIAN CONGO
BUFFALO MUSEUM OF SCIENCE (C 12621)

92   SQUATTING FETISH
FIGURE, WOOD
9½ INCHES HIGH
BENA LULUA STYLE
CENTRAL BELGIAN
CONGO
UNIVERSITY MUSEUM
PHILADELPHIA
(AF 5184)

93   STANDING FETISH
FIGURE, WOOD
10 INCHES HIGH
BASONGE STYLE
CENTRAL BELGIAN
CONGO
UNIVERSITY MUSEUM
PHILADELPHIA (AF 5194)

94 STANDING FETISH
FIGURE, WOOD
7 INCHES HIGH
BASONGE STYLE
CENTRAL BELGIAN
CONGO
COLLECTION DR. RALPH
LINTON, NEW HAVEN
CONN.

95   CUP CARVED AS
ENTIRE FIGURE, WOOD
CA. 7 INCHES HIGH
BASONGE STYLE
CENTRAL BELGIAN
CONGO
PEABODY MUSEUM
HARVARD UNIVERSITY
(B 1598)

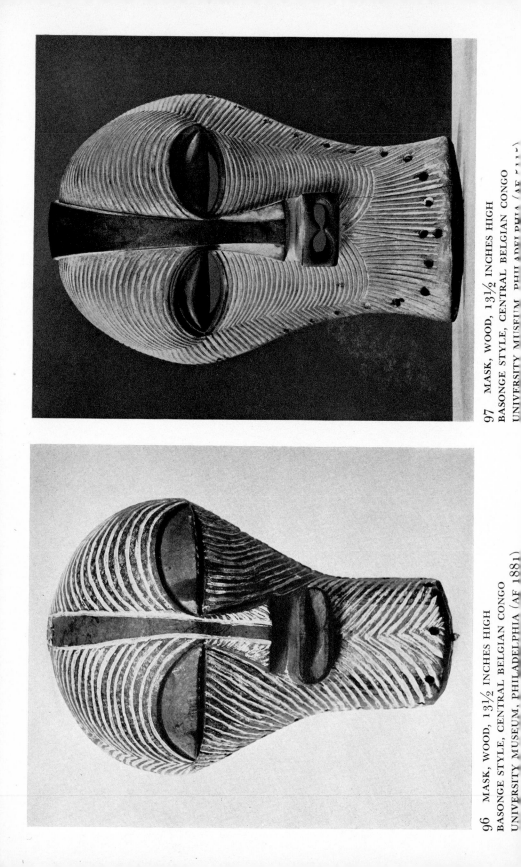

97 MASK, WOOD, 13½ INCHES HIGH
BASONGE STYLE, CENTRAL BELGIAN CONGO
UNIVERSITY MUSEUM, PHILADELPHIA (AF 511)

96 MASK, WOOD, 13½ INCHES HIGH
BASONGE STYLE, CENTRAL BELGIAN CONGO
UNIVERSITY MUSEUM, PHILADELPHIA (AF 1881)

99 MASK, WOOD, 16 INCHES HIGH
BASONGE STYLE, CENTRAL BELGIAN CONGO
BUFFALO MUSEUM OF SCIENCE (C 13728)

98 ROUND MASK, WOOD, 17 INCHES HIGH
BASONGE-BALUBA STYLE, CENTRAL BELGIAN CONGO
BUFFALO MUSEUM OF SCIENCE (C 12776)

100   STOOL WITH FEMALE FIGURE AS SUPPORT, WOOD, CA. 20 INCHES HIGH
BENA KANIOKA STYLE (?), CENTRAL BELGIAN CONGO
PEABODY MUSEUM, HARVARD UNIVERSITY (17–41–50/B 1568)

101   SEATED FEMALE FIGURE HOLDING BOWL (KABILA), WOOD, 12½ INCHES HIGH
BALUBA STYLE, SOUTHEASTERN BELGIAN CONGO
UNIVERSITY MUSEUM, PHILADELPHIA (AF 5120)

102 STOOL WITH FEMALE FIGURE AS SUPPORT, WOOD, 17 INCHES HIGH
BALUBA STYLE, SOUTHEASTERN BELGIAN CONGO
UNIVERSITY MUSEUM, PHILADELPHIA (AF 5121)

103   WATER PIPE CARVED WITH FEMALE FIGURE, WOOD, 22 INCHES HIGH
BALUBA STYLE, SOUTHEASTERN BELGIAN CONGO
BROOKLYN MUSEUM (22.1108)

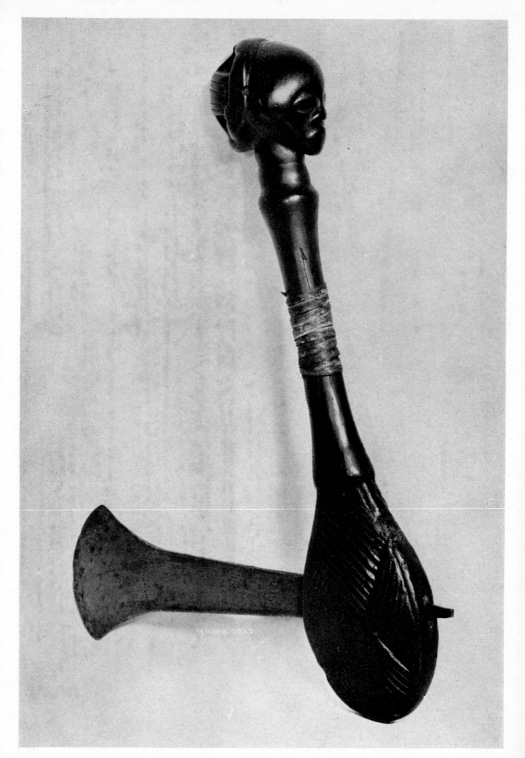

104   CEREMONIAL AXE DECORATED WITH CARVED HEAD, WOOD AND IRON
CA. 12 INCHES LONG, BLADE 9½ INCHES LONG
BALUBA STYLE, SOUTHEASTERN BELGIAN CONGO
ROYAL ONTARIO MUSEUM OF ARCHAEOLOGY, TORONTO (HAC.26)

105   NECK-REST SUPPORTED BY SQUATTING FEMALE FIGURE, WOOD, 5½ INCHES HIGH
BALUBA STYLE, SOUTHEASTERN BELGIAN CONGO
PEABODY MUSEUM, HARVARD UNIVERSITY (B 1567)

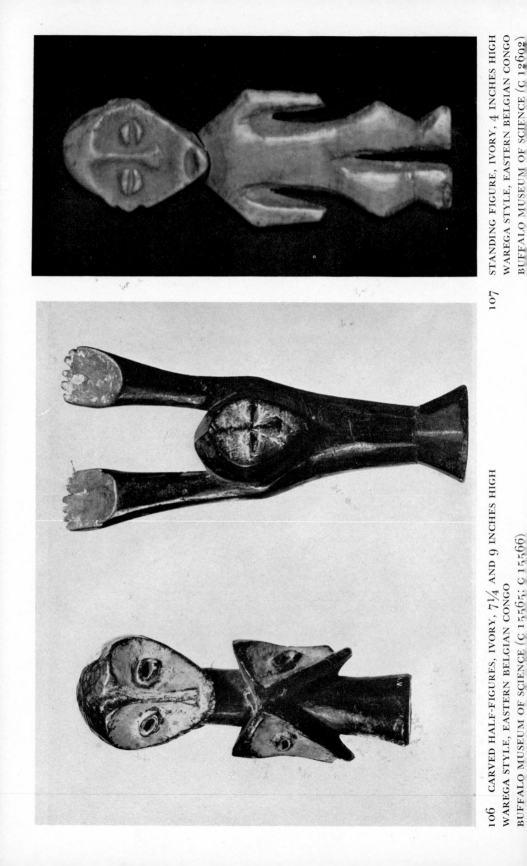

106 CARVED HALF-FIGURES, IVORY, 7¼ AND 9 INCHES HIGH
WAREGA STYLE, EASTERN BELGIAN CONGO
BUFFALO MUSEUM OF SCIENCE (C 15565; C 15566)

107 STANDING FIGURE, IVORY, 4 INCHES HIGH
WAREGA STYLE, EASTERN BELGIAN CONGO
BUFFALO MUSEUM OF SCIENCE (C 12602)

108   MASK WITH
RAFFIA FRINGE
6½ INCHES HIGH
WAREGA STYLE
EASTERN BELGIAN
CONGO
BUFFALO MUSEUM
OF SCIENCE (C 12690)

109   STOOL WITH FIGURES AS SUPPORT, WOOD, 12 INCHES HIGH
BADJOKWE STYLE, SOUTHERN CONGO-ANGOLA
BUFFALO MUSEUM OF SCIENCE (C 12714)

110   NECK-REST SUPPORTED BY STANDING FEMALE FIGURE, WOOD, 6 INCHES HIGH
BALUBA-BADJOKWE STYLE, SOUTHERN CONGO-ANGOLA
ROYAL ONTARIO MUSEUM OF ARCHAEOLOGY, TORONTO (HA.644)

111   SNUFFBOX AS FEMALE FIGURE SEATED ON CHAIR, WOOD, 5½ INCHES HIGH
BADJOKWE STYLE, SOUTHERN CONGO-ANGOLA
BROOKLYN MUSEUM (22.1089)

112 STOOL WITH TWO TIERS OF FIGURES AS SUPPORT, WOOD, $13\frac{1}{4}$ INCHES HIGH
BADJOKWE STYLE, SOUTHERN CONGO-ANGOLA
ROYAL ONTARIO MUSEUM OF ARCHAEOLOGY, TORONTO (HAC.392)

113   STAFF WITH CARVED HEAD; COMB WITH DECORATED HEAD, WOOD, 18 INCHES LONG; 7 INCHES HIGH
BADJOKWE STYLE, SOUTHERN CONGO-ANGOLA
ROYAL ONTARIO MUSEUM OF ARCHAEOLOGY, TORONTO (HA.506; HAC.339,578)

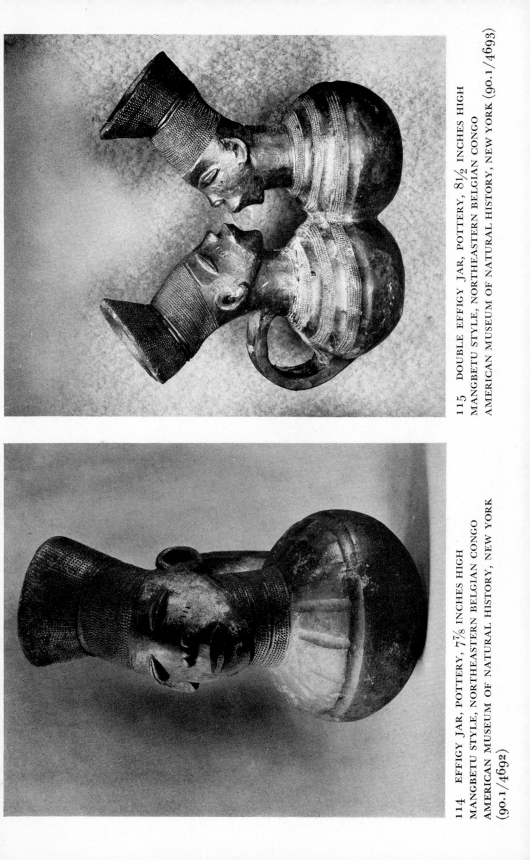

115 DOUBLE EFFIGY JAR, POTTERY, 8½ INCHES HIGH
MANGBETU STYLE, NORTHEASTERN BELGIAN CONGO
AMERICAN MUSEUM OF NATURAL HISTORY, NEW YORK (90.1/4693)

114 EFFIGY JAR, POTTERY, 7⅞ INCHES HIGH
MANGBETU STYLE, NORTHEASTERN BELGIAN CONGO
AMERICAN MUSEUM OF NATURAL HISTORY, NEW YORK
(90.1/4692)

116   CYLINDRICAL BOX
WITH CARVED HEAD
WOOD AND BARK
CA. 20 INCHES HIGH
MANGBETU STYLE
NORTHEASTERN
BELGIAN CONGO
PEABODY MUSEUM
HARVARD UNIVERSITY
(B 1591)